JET LIBRARY

FRAGILE LIVES
Death, Dying And Care

FRAGILE LIVES

Death, dying and care

Beverley McNamara

OPEN UNIVERSITY PRESS
Buckingham • Philadelphia

Open University Press
Celtic Court
22 Ballmoor
Buckingham
MK18 1XW

email: enquiries@openup.co.uk
world wide web: www.openup.co.uk

and
325 Chestnut Street
Philadelphia, PA 19106, USA

First published in 2001

A catalogue record of this book is available from the British Library

ISBN 0335 20899 1

Library of Congress Cataloging-in-Publication Data available

Set in 11/12 pt Bembo by DOCUPRO, Canberra
Printed by South Wind Productions, Singapore

Contents

Preface

The initiative for this book came out of the many conversations I have had with my friend and mentor Charles Waddell. Charles has never turned away from researching and writing about sensitive and emotive topics, like dying and death, and from him I have learned to face these topics with courage and good humour. Allan Kellehear's important and continuing work on Australian approaches to dying and death has also been a source of inspiration and example for my own work. As I argue in this book, learning about how people die requires us to examine our own inadequacies and frailties. The fragile lives I write about in the book are therefore not just those of terminally ill patients, they are also the fragile lives we all inherit through birth. In exploring this fragility, I have drawn upon the stories provided by many terminally ill people, their families and the health professionals who cared for them in their last days and months. With their kind permission, I have changed their names and located their individual stories within the social and cultural context of contemporary Western society. While I use Australian case studies, I believe these are reflective of broader trends in multicultural Western societies. The euthanasia debate and the development of palliative care are issues of global importance, and public debate surrounding dying and death is informed by an increasingly globalised media. A large part of this book is devoted to a discussion of the care of terminally ill people, but I have sought, above all, to emphasise the experience of those who lived through the process of dying. It is painful to witness the suffering of those who are dying, but it is beyond imagination to undertake that dreaded journey ourselves.

This book does not provide ready solutions to the complex social, ethical and philosophical problems that are evident in the area of terminal care. However, by framing life stories and clinical dramas within contemporary social theory, I do raise a number of questions that require us to search for possible ways we can manage dying in a sensitive and socially responsible manner. I have not shied away from demonstrating how difficult the contemporary management of dying is, and I have set out to illustrate that dying is a chaotic and uncertain process. Yet, despite the disorderly manner in which people die, social and cultural patterns can be found in the way that we approach dying and the care of terminally ill people. These patterns reassure us that we are social creatures who share the burden of dying and that we can look to one another for guidance in facing our inevitable deaths.

There are many people who have helped in enabling my research and in the writing of this book. Most importantly, I wish to thank the terminally ill people and their family members who appear in the following pages. Only fragments of their lives appear, but through these fragments their fears and concerns echo a terror we all feel. I have enormous respect for the health professionals who work in the important area of terminal care and I am particularly grateful to the palliative care professionals who have supported my work. Although it is always difficult to isolate individuals, I wish to acknowledge the help of Ellen Nightingale, Kevin Yuen and Karen Martin, who assisted me throughout the period of my research in Perth hospice and palliative care services. I have benefited most from the encouragement and wisdom of Charles Waddell, who has maintained a continuing interest in my work. For intellectual guidance and written comment, I wish to thank Alan Petersen, Allan Kellehear, David Field and David Clark. My colleagues and students in the Department of Anthropology at The University of Western Australia, particularly Victoria Burbank, have offered continuing stimulation, support and friendship. Thanks to Anna Wildy who helped with many of the last minute details of manuscript preparation. Elizabeth Weiss from Allen & Unwin has maintained a steadfast support for this project and Judy Waters has provided incisive editorial advice and encouragement.

I have been enriched and humbled by witnessing the terminal illness and death of my own father, Eddie. Lex, John, Julia, Meagan and Glyn deserve my unending gratitude as, without their love and support, I could never have completed this book.

one

Life in the face of death

Dying is something most of us would rather not think about. The idea of death is frightening, casting a shadow of constraint upon us all. This shadow is not just something that we bear as individuals, for 'dying' is a social problem. The totality of social organisation and human culture relates to survival and to pushing back the moment of death through focusing on the worth of living (Bauman 1992). Death interrupts the human achievement of living with no thought of finality, reminding us all of our shared fragility. I propose, in the chapters that follow, that we acknowledge this shared fragility, for the individual alone and in terror shatters in the process of dying. This book examines the process of dying and how we care for dying people, for in doing this, and in acknowledging our fragile lives, we are strengthened by the human bond. At the point of death, we are beyond the ministrations of others, but while we are dying it is imperative that we, in some small way, are part of social life. The care of terminally ill people is therefore much more than a health care issue that necessitates a workforce of compassionate health professionals. We need to see the context of terminal care as a microcosm reflective of important global issues. Some of the most important social, philosophical and ethical issues are evident in the stories of ordinary men and women who die each day and in the stories of the health professionals who care for them.

This book is based primarily on the stories of people close to death in one of two ways. Through exploring the experiences of terminally ill people and their families, we are reminded of the ways that lives are brought to the point of breaking, though intricate facades are often created to hide the underlying fragility and despair. Another group of people come close to death through their work, which finds them face to face with despair, grief and pain. In the stories of the health professionals who care for dying people, and in those of people I have known who have died, I have been prompted to frame the human problem of dying in sociological ways. It is important to make clear the connections between the individual and society for 'how death is met, understood and dealt with practically, arises from the social patterns and perceptions that inform that society' (Ballard 1996, p. 7). By acknowledging the social and cultural context of dying and death, we are better able to address those social, philosophical and ethical questions which complicate the dying process. We are also better able to face the idea of death ourselves because we are better informed and better prepared for the messiness, the overwhelming grief and the suffering associated with dying. Dying has always challenged humankind, but in an age of uncertainty, of increasing individualism and multicultural diversity, the 'language of death' is no longer the 'communal language of religion' (Walter 1994, p. 9). Dying in contemporary Western society is therefore a challenge which highlights the fragile nature of mind, body and spirit. As a society, we need to meet this challenge, understand the roots of uncertainty, and celebrate the nature of diverse social and cultural life, for we continue to live on in the face of death.

Dying is an uncertain process, but there are also patterns evident in the ways that people die in contemporary Western society. People, on average, now live longer and many have a high quality of life throughout the course of their lives. Life expectation at birth has increased in the United Kingdom, the United States of America and Australia. In the United Kingdom in 1994, life expectation at birth was 73.9 years for men and 79.2 for women (Government Statistical Service (UK) 1999), figures that are comparable to the United States where in 1995 life expectation at birth was 72.5 years for men and 79.3 for women (United States Census Bureau 1997). The dramatic changes that have taken place are demonstrated in Australian data where, in the period 1901–10 a newborn boy was expected to live to 55.2 years and a newborn girl to 58.8 years. Over the course of approximately 90 years, the life expectancy of men has increased by 20 years, while for women it has increased by 22 years (Australian Bureau of Statistics 2000). Women are now far less likely to die in childbirth and babies are expected to survive infancy. Public health and diet have improved and medical technology has afforded us greater protection from disease. This means that death normally comes after a reasonably long life, but when we do die, we die of different diseases than those that claimed the lives of our ancestors. Many of us will experience a prolonged dying through the ravages of cancer and heart disease. Demographic changes coupled with increasing life-supporting and life-enhancing technology result—somewhat paradoxically—in extended life *and* extended dying. The phenomenon of prolonged dying has many implications for us all, but particularly for the health professionals who specialise in the care of terminally ill people. These professionals are at the coalface of death, on the one hand wielding enormous power, yet on the other humbled by the inevitable presence of death. Health professionals who care for dying people are inescapably confronted with the problem of dying—though the problem, of course, belongs to us all.

Although we are not consciously aware of it, much of our cultural and social life is spent dealing with the problem of death. At a social level, this problem is more evident at different times and in different places. Obviously dying and death pose greater challenges when people die in huge numbers, at an early age or in particularly tragic circumstances. Studies of how people deal with death also indicate that in certain historical times death takes on greater social significance. From a contemporary perspective, we know that after World War II changes took place in Western societies; most often, dying people were taken from their families to hospitals to die in a clinical environment (Aries 1974; Blauner 1966). Prior to the war, which made grief an all too common experience, families often tended to their terminally ill relatives in their own homes (Gorer 1965). After World War II, people became less used to the sight of dying people and, because they were no longer familiar, dying and death became awkward and even embarrassing for both the dying person and the other people who looked on and later grieved privately (Elias 1985). The 'baby boomer generation' know little about dying people. As a child in the 1960s, I was not permitted to attend my grandmother's funeral; the suicide of a neighbour was kept from me; and the death of a young friend of the family in a motor vehicle accident was whispered about, with my mother sitting for hours over a blank sympathy card.

The modern hospice movement, founded in 1967 (Stoddard 1978), and framed within a broader 'death awareness' movement (Metcalf & Huntington 1991), brought much-needed attention to the care of dying people. A few influential people, like Cicely Saunders, who established the hospice movement (du Boulay 1984; Clark 1998), and Elisabeth Kubler-Ross, who wrote the seminal book *On Death and Dying* (1969), drew attention to the plight of dying people in Western societies. Some of these dying people were neglected and left to die lonely and in pain. Others became the 'objects' of medical experimentation as new technologies were developed and changed at an alarming rate. The philosophy associated with the hospice movement proposed that dying and death were a part of life that need not be feared and should be discussed openly. Dying people, it was thought, should be allowed to die peacefully, surrounded by their families and friends and unencumbered by invasive technology. Through the work of those involved in the hospice movement and in the development of palliative care, improvements have been made in the relief of pain and the delivery of sensitive and humane care. Yet, despite these changes, the extent to which people have shown more acceptance and less fear of death is debatable. Medicine continues to be driven by a technological imperative. Expensive machinery and stocks of drugs stand as a testament to the power of technology in hospitals around the world to ward off death—or at the very least, to minimise its biological sting. Recent worldwide interest in euthanasia, otherwise known as the 'requested death' movement (McInerney 2000), again draws attention to the problem of death and the discomfort we feel when faced with the indignities of dying a prolonged death.

Undoubtedly the contemporary pursuit of individualism and the postmodern nature of Western society, which exemplifies a multiplicity of beliefs and practices, can give many of us opportunities to explore different options for our living and dying. Seale (1998) has even argued that the human social bond continues in the face of death and is enacted through a variety of cultural scripts that emanate from medicine, psychology and the media. However, while individual choice is now heralded as a moral ethic, clinical, social, existential and moral uncertainties temper both the care of terminally ill people and the act of dying itself. No one is free to choose the death they would wish and it may be a blessing that we do not know what is in store for us. Nevertheless, some of us are better able to control the circumstances of our own deaths. If we are incapacitated by pain and fatigue and cognitively impaired by disease, we will have little strength and ability to choose how we will be cared for. If we are from a non-English speaking background, if our social networks are weak, and if we have little money and access to power, who will listen to our requests for a 'good death'? All of the chapters in this book acknowledge the 'messiness' of death, its unpredictability and capacity to intensify our fragility, for our lives are fragile in the face of death.

> Man's consciously lived frailty, individuality and relatedness make the experience of pain, of sickness and of death an integral part of his life. The ability to cope with this trio autonomously is fundamental to his health (Illich 1976 p. 169).

As Illich notes, acknowledging our frailty in the face of death is a way of making our societies and ourselves healthier.

DYING AND DEATH IN HISTORICAL AND CULTURAL CONTEXT

I have suggested that dying is a social problem. In order to understand how we manage this problem, we need to review the ways in which death is managed at different times and in different places. Comparison allows us to generalise and isolate the particular. How then are we similar to, or different from, our ancestors or even our parents, and how do we manage dying differently from other cultures? Through an extensive literature drawn from anthropology, sociology, history, philosophy and social psychology, we find that dying is not simply a biological fact but a social process, and death not a moment in time, but a social phenomenon. The ways in which dying and death are understood have implications for individuals and societies alike, and we cannot assume that behaviours evoked by death are solely in response to a biological fact.

> Death provides occasions and materials for a symbolic discourse on life—through the different treatments accorded to those whose lives have ended in different ways and at different stages of development, through theories about the afterlife, through symbols used in funerary rites or eschatology [doctrines of the last or final things] to express the contrast between life and death (Humphreys & King 1981, pp. 9–10).

However, the conditions of modern Western living mean that the search for a symbolic discourse on life or death is fraught with difficulty. We live in a world in which, through the process of globalisation, we share a great deal of information, yet we are strangers to one another. Our societies are multicultural and diverse, our families for the most part are nuclear and mobile, and our communities are no longer restricted to a specific locale. However, if there is a universal measure or impact of death, as anthropologists Metcalf and Huntington (1991, p. 24) suggest, perhaps it is in the *way* that death becomes a social problem. Berger (1967, pp. 43–44) suggests that, as 'the knowledge of death cannot be avoided in any society, legitimations of the reality of the social world *in the face of death* are decisive requirements in any society' (emphasis as in the original).

Within any single society or time period, the concerns of one individual will never be reproduced by another. Yet in some societies and time periods, shared ideas about life, death and the after-life are more clearly articulated than in others. Cross-cultural studies depict a variety of responses to dying and death which, at first sight, seem to have little in common. However, perhaps the most salient aspect of many anthropological studies about death is the way in which ritual works to ascribe meaning to death for both individuals and the social collectivity (Hertz 1960; Bloch & Parry 1982; Metcalf & Huntington 1991). Whether custom calls for celebratory or restrained behaviour, whether we turn to religious doctrine or create our own 'spirituality', dying and death provide opportunities for people to evaluate life experience. Several scholars have proposed that the breakdown of ritual in contemporary Western society has led to a general discomfort with the reality of death. Elias (1985, p. 27) suggests that modern people distrust ritual, while Gorer (1965) argues that World War II marked the decline of formal rituals for mourning in Britain which led to the decline of norms to guide people through dying, death and bereavement. The privatisation of dying and death is evident in the chapters that follow and in our own responses to the subject. Rarely are dying and death public events, though there are always exceptions—as we know from the public displays of grief at the death of Princess Diana.

Aries (1974, 1981), a French social historian, suggests that, until recently, death in Western societies was a social phenomenon in which communal responses were expressed through distinctive signs and ritual. Death in the pre-modern era was, according to Aries, 'tame', whereas death in contemporary times is so 'savage' and terrible that it is ultimately hidden or denied. This modern 'savagery' creeps in under the mask of medical technology and the death of the patient in the hospital, covered with tubes, becomes 'a popular image, more terrifying than the *transi* or skeleton of macabre rhetoric' (1981, p. 614). Aries' claims have not been accepted unconditionally, with Elias (1985) suggesting that this nostalgic view is overly romantic. Assumptions that death was in some sense more 'natural' in traditional societies draw heavily upon the myth of the 'noble savage' (Walter 1995). Non-Western death rituals are often presented within frames of reference specific to Western discourses (Hockey 1996). Hockey proposes that therapy-oriented practices that derive from academic observations are liable to distort cultural and individual responses to dying and death. These observations are particularly pertinent in the context of multicultural societies, where—as will be evident in various chapters throughout the book—dying people and their families draw upon non-Western as well as Western cultural views.

CONTEMPORARY RESPONSES TO DYING AND DEATH

We cannot avoid noting the changes in Western societies that now leave most of us bereft of ritual and religious meaning and increasingly reliant upon rational scientific approaches to dying and death. Dying and death in contemporary Western society are now more private than in earlier historical periods, yet paradoxically they are also less within the control of the individual and his or her close social network. Dying generally takes place within the confines of the hospital, and both dying and death are regulated by the state and subsumed within scientific discourses (Prior 1989). The increasing privatisation, secularisation and medicalisation of dying and death have been subject to ongoing critique. For Blauner (1966), the equilibrium of the group is paramount and though specific deaths disrupt the functioning of the social system and are heavily medicalised, the group ultimately restores the 'social fabric' through custom and norms (1966, p. 394). This theoretical position has been overshadowed by more recent sociological attempts to explain death within present-day postmodern society which is multifaceted, complex and prone to division (Elias 1985; Bauman 1992; Walter 1994). Despite the obvious complexity of contemporary society, Blauner's proposal that the impact of mortality is related to the demographic characteristics of a society is compelling. As I have already noted, people in contemporary Western societies are more likely to die in old age than at birth or in middle age, which means that death can often pass unnoticed. The elderly have ceased to contribute markedly to economic production and culturally society tends to focus upon youth, health and fitness. With the increase in long-term chronic illnesses, the majority of deaths are medicalised. The certainty of approaching death for the chronically ill person, then, tends to develop slowly over a long period of time (Field 1996).

Mellor and Schilling (1993) have argued that death has become privatised due to the individuals' reordering of constructions of self and the changing scope of the sacred in society. Death, therefore, is 'sequestrated' or hidden from public view and becomes a technical matter to be dealt with by experts (Giddens 1991, pp. 161–62). The decline of religious belief in Western contemporary society is directly implicated in this argument. The good death that was made possible by religion (Berger 1967, p. 44) is now less possible. Consequently, survival strategies of self-care that construe death as an individual event replace the collective strategy of religion as a means of dealing with the constant awareness of death (Bauman 1992). According to Bauman, a major feature of this survival strategy is the individual's concern with health and fitness of the body. It seems that, in our pursuit of health, we push death away, but inevitably death approaches and it does so in a specific historical and cultural context. Our awareness of this context helps us to locate our own individual responses within a framework of society; as members of society we see that we are all affected by death and that, though frightening, death comes to us all.

It seems that the secularisation, privatisation and medicalisation of society are forces that play off one another, creating tensions that are articulated in paradoxes of uncertainty and technical rationality. Individuals may be uncertain of how to behave when they are dying, or when a loved one is dying; uncertainty exists in relation to belief in an afterlife;

and possibilities for an afterlife go beyond the boundaries of conventional religious belief to encompass an eclectic spiritual dimension which borrows from various cultural sources, including the emerging New Age discourses. Medical science, which is driven by a technological imperative to manage health, illness and death (Bates & Lapsley 1985; Freund & McGuire 1991), offers one counter-argument to uncertainty, and the public health movement, which stresses health promotion and risk management, proposes another (Lupton 1995). Societal preoccupations with individuality further complicate present attitudes to death, creating a situation whereby the focus on the individual's wishes becomes a moral and ethical imperative (Kellehear 1996, p. 89).

Walter (1994) proposes a 'postmodern revival' of death which incorporates personal experience and 'places private feelings firmly onto the public agenda' (1994, p. 41). As society has become more complex, Walter suggests that public discourse about dying and death has become fragmented. The public is now far more willing to challenge the authority of medical experts. I believe this wave of dissatisfaction with the power and limitations of medicine does not come just from the public, and that many within the health professional community share some of this dissatisfaction. For example, discussions surrounding euthanasia in many Western countries have become part of popular media and everyday conversation. Professional reappraisals of medicine's role in the management of dying have also been clearly articulated in the rhetoric of the hospice and palliative care movement. I discuss the hospice and palliative care movement in detail in many parts of this book, in particular in Chapter 10. However, it is worth noting here how influential hospice and palliative care have been in drawing attention to dying people who have either been neglected in their suffering or forced to face an undignified and overly medicalised death. Nevertheless, in keeping with the nature of postmodern society, even social movements like hospice and palliative care are subject to the forces of social change. As such, they do not necessarily reflect a consistent philosophical and political stance, as will become evident throughout this book.

The contemporary approaches to dying and death, which include the hospice and palliative care movement and the 'requested death' (euthanasia) movement (McInerney 2000), challenge the idea that death is a taboo subject and give weight to previous sociological critique of this notion (Kellehear 1984; Walter 1991, 1994). Armstrong (1987) challenges the silence surrounding dying and death by demonstrating that the death certificate has served as a professionally managed symbol of death within the public domain since the mid-nineteenth century. Dying and death are, however, still most often discussed theoretically in moral and ethical tones in public, in a clinical and supposedly objective sense in the professional arena, and on a 'need to know' basis in the private realm.

Both the public and private realms engage in the scientific discourse promulgated by medicine, although there is an increasing tendency in both public and private realms to use various cultural forms to explain and manage death. In this way, an array of verbal and non-verbal texts and action surrounding dying and death are the outcome of knowledge engendered by both professional and lay people alike. It also seems apparent that, while dying and death have become legitimate topics for open discussion, there is no high degree of community consensus on the way dying and death are managed. The medical establishment, parliaments and communities are divided in opinion about a number of issues surrounding dying and death. Debate ranges from whether euthanasia should be made available to issues of funding and provision for high technology intensive care, as well as for palliative care services.

The multicultural nature of many Western societies adds further variation to community perceptions regarding end-of-life decision-making (Waddell & McNamara 1997) and poses challenges to the delivery of culturally appropriate care to terminally ill patients (McNamara et al. 1997). In Australia, for example, where over 200 languages are spoken, the 1996 census data revealed that 16 per cent of the population spoke a language other than English at home (Australian Bureau of Statistics 2000). Many of these people, as well as the Aboriginal people of Australia, come from cultural backgrounds which continue to adhere to traditional beliefs and rituals associated with dying and death. However, despite such diversity, scientific and technical prowess and secular beliefs dominate Western societies. Illich (1976, p. 175) notes that medical technologies are not culturally neutral and that the 'white man's image of death has spread with medical civilisation and has been a major force in cultural colonisation'. In present-day Western societies, while there appears to be a focus on individuality and a new challenge to the hegemony of scientific thinking, there is also a paradoxical dependence on medicine to provide answers to social as well as medical problems (Lupton 1994). This kind of paradox is indicative of a society that is subject to both globalising influences and personal dispositions in which individual life is firmly interlaced with changing forms brought about by modern organisation (Giddens 1990, 1991). While individuals die, the impact of individual deaths continues to go beyond the realms of the personal.

FRAGILE LIVES IN THE FACE OF DEATH

Throughout this book, I argue that the inevitability of death and the way that we, as a society, deal with dying lends a poignancy and fragility to our existence. Western societies no longer rely on religion to give meaning to our common existential dilemmas and we can turn in any number of directions in our search for meaning. The following chapters explore fragile lives from a number of different perspectives. Most obvious of all fragile lives are those of dying people, whose vulnerability confronts the precarious mortality of the living. Yet we often do not realise just how fragile we all are in the face of death. I explore how individuals, social institutions and health professional cultures employ methods of control and coping that help alleviate anxiety about death. We are, as mortals, easily broken, yet despite its overarching shadow, we continue life in the face of death. In exploring issues to do with how we manage or cope with death, I discuss anthropological and sociological research I have conducted over the past six years. I am drawn to the subject of dying in an attempt to understand a social problem that motivates not just individual existential inquiry but, more importantly, the fundamental organisation of some of our major institutions. Though I refer to religious belief and the increasing secularisation of society, I focus principally upon the medical management of dying.

I use a variety of research methods to illustrate the complex and sensitive issue of dying. My early research with palliative care nurses alerted me to the enormous capacity some humans have for embracing others in times of tragedy and despair. From my initial concern with understanding how palliative care nurses coped with the stress of nursing dying people I became further interested in the hospice movement and in the development of palliative care. I conducted an extensive ethnographic study of Western Australian palliative care services in which I interviewed many health professionals and observed how they went about caring for terminally ill people and their families. This study was further informed by visits to many hospices and palliative care services and interviews with palliative care professionals in other states of Australia and in Britain, Singapore, Hong Kong and China. I conducted a survey of the public's thoughts about facing death and another of palliative care professionals' impressions of providing care in a multicultural society with my colleague Charles Waddell. Most recently, I have interviewed terminally ill people and their families from a variety of backgrounds. As most of my research was conducted in palliative care organisations, I have presented terminal illness within a specific context. Most people cared for in hospices and by palliative care services have cancer, and their terminal illness is mediated by the pain and stigma associated with this dreadful disease. These people are also more likely to receive specialised and excellent levels of supportive care compared to some who may be lost within institutionalised aged care or large impersonal hospitals. Nevertheless, my explorations of care in terminal illness have relevance to all who face the care of dying people and the thought of dying themselves.

In the next chapter I discuss how people think and talk about facing death. Survey data illustrate attitudes to euthanasia and to using an advance directive to plan for future death, whereas my material from interviews with terminally ill people and their families gives a somewhat more human view of the experience of dying. I contrast how attitudes to euthanasia reported in an impersonal survey are very different to the intimate requests or silences of those who are near to death and uncertain of where to turn. In keeping with popular notions of free will and individuality, the public often believe that euthanasia should be made available to terminally ill people, yet the realities are often ethically charged and psychologically and socially untenable. It is no simple coincidence that euthanasia requests are associated with the cancer death, and in Chapter 3 I consider the question of why cancer is so feared. Cancer is considered by some to be a death sentence and the amount of media attention given to cancer 'cures' and cancer research reflects the community's preoccupation with this disease. The implications for people dying from cancer are overwhelming and include dealing with what is regarded as a 'dirty' and insidious disease, as well as coping with levels of certainty and uncertainty associated with the progression and treatment of cancer. The process of 'living dying' is a frighteningly real prospect for us all, as cancer is now the leading cause of death in many countries around the world, including Australia, Canada, Italy, Japan, the Netherlands, New Zealand, the United Kingdom and the United States of America (World Health Organisation 1996).

With the very real prospect of dying over a prolonged period through cancer or other end-stage diseases, we may need to reinterpret the fragility of our lives so that we can die a 'good' death. In Chapter 4 I consider a number of different constructions of a good death, most specifically those that have been proposed within the hospice and palliative care movement. This chapter considers the arguments that propose we should bring death out into the open and those that focus on respect for the rights of each individual to write their own scripts for dying (Walter 1994; Seale 1998). However, it is not as if we can plan our own 'good death', and in Chapter 5 I show how some people are more fragile when faced with death due to a number of physical, sociological and personal factors. I use case studies to explore how disease status, religious belief, ethnicity, social class, gender and social support mediate the experience of dying. Most significantly, our experience of dying will, in all probability, be framed within the context of medicine, and in Chapter 6 I focus on the vital functional and symbolic role that medicine plays in the social management of death. Despite the over-whelming fascination that medicine has with the salvational technology associated with prolonging life, we can still find a variety of practices within the medical community which show resistance to the prominent theory that medicine should 'save' humans from death.

Over the past century, secrecy about dying has prevented many people in Western societies from speaking openly about their approaching deaths and until very recently doctors and other health professionals were complicit in this denial. Chapter 7 details how new practices which encourage the open disclosure of the diagnosis and prognosis are now challenged by the realities of working in a multicultural society. Versions of the truth about dying must therefore be negotiated within a framework of social relationships rather than universal bioethics. The broader context of ethical practice is also discussed in Chapter 8, where I discuss the topical issues of patient autonomy and professional control in terminal illness and care. I argue that patient autonomy, while highly valued in individualistic Western societies, is conditional upon a number of factors which lie outside the patient's control. Professional control is often contrasted with patient autonomy, yet—as my discussion highlights—both control and autonomy are negotiated within complex situational settings. The complexity of professional work in terminal care is further illustrated in Chapter 9, where I discuss the rewards and costs of caring for dying people. It is not just dying people who are fragile; the people who care for them, who stay with them through pain and sorrow and who truly have an intimate knowledge of the terror and loneliness of dying, are also fragile in the face of death. With the advent of hospice, and more recently of palliative care and palliative medicine, health professionals have drawn attention to the special needs of dying people and their families. In the final chapter I focus on how the process of specialisation in dying and death, facilitated through palliative care, may in fact begin to mask death by concentrating on the medical aspects of dying.

CONCLUSION

> Life is a fragile commodity, frequently undervalued by those able to enjoy a good quality of life who live in the belief that 'it will never happen to me' . . . Whilst able to enjoy life and thinking, it is hard to imagine a world as it continues and in which, as individuals, we cease to exist. However, death is no respecter of age, creed or social class, and frequently cuts people off in their prime (Finlay 1996, pp. 74–75).

This chapter, and indeed the entire book, is designed to provide some background against which we can make sense of our own dying. It is essential that the people who are involved in the care of terminally ill people and those who have a general interest in the management of terminal care make sense of death by facing the possibility of it themselves. We need not face death in the literal sense, but we need to face the idea of it for in acknowledging death we acknowledge life in the face of death. Our empathy and our own vulnerability, then, are mirrors of a shared humanity to those who must die before us. As Nuland (1993, p. 268) argues, 'the classic image of dying with dignity must be modified or even discarded', but we must give some kind of hope for those we leave behind. The hope and the message to others is that the dignity 'we seek in dying must be found in the dignity with which we have lived our lives'.

The lesson that life goes on in the face of death was brought home to me most strongly the day that my father died. After sitting by his bed for some time, then packing up his few small things from the drawers and cupboards in the hospice room, we drove home, stopping along the way to buy fish and chips. The family gathered to eat the impromptu meal and I could not help but feel guilty that we ate while Dad had died. How could we eat fish and chips when he could not join us for his favourite meal? We ate, did the washing up, slept and continued to live our lives in much the same way as we had done before, diminished by his absence but strengthened by his memory and the experience of grief. I heard another example of 'fish and chip' philosophy told by a Mandy, a palliative care nurse, in a gathering where nurses and doctors were exchanging 'funny but tragic' stories. Mandy was asked to visit an elderly couple because Mrs Weeks could not manage to wake Mr Weeks and 'his fish and chips were getting cold'. Mandy suspected that Mr Weeks had finally died in his sleep after months of terminal cancer. On arriving, she found Mr Weeks dead but under a huge pile of blankets on the bed, his small wizened face peacefully at rest. Mrs Weeks explained that he was cold and that she had tried to warm him up. When Mandy broke the news to her she could only say: 'But who will eat the fish and chips—do you want some?'

In order to find meaning in both life and death, we need to feed the body and nourish social communion with one another so that we may continue to live on in the face of death.

two

Thoughts about facing death

No matter how zealously you drink your orange juice, eat your fruit and vegetables, organise your sleep and do your exercises, the fact remains that one day you will be dead. The only question though, given current medical technologies, by no means a trivial one, is when. The present controversy rages around the notion that you should be able to decide this for yourself, especially if you find yourself in the advanced stages of an apparently soon-to-be-fatal illness (Anonymous 1997, p. 21).

Death does not hold great appeal as a topic of discussion, but the extent to which it is considered taboo is debatable (Gorer 1965; Aries 1981). People do think and talk about facing death (Kastenbaum 1988; Walter 1991; Littlewood 1993), as evidenced in the array of literature presented for public consumption (Kellehear 1990) and the growing number of death-related resources on the Internet (Hewitt 1996). We only have to turn on the television set to be confronted with scenes of death brought to us through live coverage of ethnic cleansing and natural disasters. Thoughts about death are no doubt present, though thoughts about facing one's own death arise in very specific contexts, and usually in one of two ways. First, healthy people who have no personal experience of someone close to them dying do not dwell on death, and when they do give some thought to the subject it is usually in abstract terms, devoid of the emotional edge of suffering associated with terminal illness. People who are terminally ill, and their loved ones, give voice to a second level of discussion, which is heavily laden with confusion and fear. They are often less certain about end-of-life matters than healthy people who are untouched by death, because terminally ill people and their families are faced with a very real future loss.

The contrast between healthy people's thoughts about facing death and those of terminally ill people can be demonstrated by drawing upon two kinds of data. A survey I conducted with Charles Waddell (1997) illustrates attitudes to euthanasia and the use of an advance directive to plan for future death. Observational research and interviews with dying people and their families, by way of contrast, give a more intimate understanding of how people actually think about approaching death. While the survey study indicates trends in public opinion about dying and death, the face-to-face discussions collectively portray the uncertainties and changing circumstances of dying people and their families. Attitudes to euthanasia reported in an impersonal survey are very different from the intimate requests or silences of those who are near to death. In keeping with popular notions of free will and individuality, the public often believe that euthanasia should be made available to terminally ill people, yet the realities are often ethically charged and psychologically and socially untenable. However, we must keep the debate open; while the philosophical questions about death cannot be answered, we cannot refuse to ask them. A lack of curiosity about death diminishes our humanity, but equally, thinking about death brings to the fore our shared fragility.

The uncertainties associated with facing death are not necessarily confined to contemporary times. However, as the influential sociologist Anthony Giddens (1991) suggests, the pre-modern world was characterised by a widespread acceptance of notions of fate and fortune. In contrast, the contemporary age has an obsession with monitoring risk, a mechanism that supposedly keeps doubt and consequent anxieties under control (Elias 1985; Bauman 1992; Beck 1992). Giddens argues that all cultures share a practical consciousness, whereby feelings of ontological insecurity are bracketed off, enabling individuals to carry out their day-to-day activities without an open awareness of chaos. In other words, we find that most people are more likely to monitor their diet and exercise in order to prevent life-threatening illnesses than simply accept a terminal diagnosis as their fate. People think about living for as long as possible rather than living in preparation for an after-life: 'We are beginning to react to death as we would to a communicable disease . . . [it] is coming to be seen as the consequence of personal neglect or untoward accident.' (Fulton 1965, p. 4). Gorer (1965, p. 114) proposes that the outcome of waging a war against the causes of death is an 'excessive preoccupation with the risk of death'. Implicit in this preoccupation is the notion that we can do more than simply replace one cause of death for another—if we can eliminate all risks, we will be immortal. This, of course, is not the case and many people do face terminal illnesses while others witness their loved ones succumb to terminal illnesses and die. Thoughts about facing death, in these contexts, are very different from the ideas expressed by relatively healthy people who are asked to respond to questions about dying and death. Healthy people bracket off the immediate reality and chaos of death and formulate ideas from a supposedly 'rational' position.

THE PUBLIC AND MEDICAL DEBATE

Recent public debate on euthanasia and decision-making at the end of life heralds a new phase of public awareness about dying and death. While euthanasia is an ancient concept, decriminalisation and legislative proce-dures regarding the various forms of assisted death are contemporary issues of global interest and importance. End-of-life issues now require inter-vention beyond medicine and lawyers and politicians join doctors in the ranks of key players who feature strongly in public discussions. However, even if we can accept that dying and death have become legitimate topics for discussion, we cannot pronounce a high degree of community consensus on issues surrounding dying and death. Within the communi-ties represented in Western societies, several voices beg to be heard and these range from an array of 'rational' and ethically 'correct' arguments to plaintive pleas that echo fear, disempowerment and suffering.

The medical establishment, parliaments and lay communities are divided in opinion about the manner in which terminal illness and the process of dying are managed. The Netherlands is often taken to be the pioneering jurisdiction of law reform regarding medical aid in dying. However, euthanasia remains a criminal offence in this country, though various sections within the Dutch Criminal Code allow doctors to administer medical aid to dying people under specific guidelines (Pappas 1996, p. 170). The Dutch value the concept of patient self-determination through reducing the blame placed upon doctors who support those who request assistance in dying. Nevertheless, in other Western countries where patient self-determination and autonomy are also valued, doctors who help their patients to die are not looked upon with favour. America's contro-versial Dr Jack Kevorkian, nicknamed Doctor Death, was not supported in his campaign to assist terminally ill people to die and in April 1999 was convicted of second-degree murder. A Michigan judge sentenced Kevorkian to between ten and 25 years in prison (*Frontline* 1999).

Australia became a testing ground for euthanasia legislation when, for nine months between July 1996 and March 1997, euthanasia became legally available for the first time in the world. This form of assisted death was provided, subject to strict medical monitoring, to a select few individuals in the Northern Territory of Australia (Kissane et al. 1998). However, the *Rights of the Terminally Ill Act* 1996 was short lived. The Australian Senate responded to various anti-euthanasia political pressures, articulated most prominently by the prime minister of Australia, John Howard, and overturned the Territory's legislation (Rose 1997; Quirk 1998). Howard went against popular opinion as, over the past three decades, public opinion polls in Australia have confirmed that the majority of Australians are in favour of active voluntary euthanasia (Roy Morgan Research Centre 1996). Debate was particularly lively in the time before and during the Northern Territory *Rights of the Terminally Ill Act*, with most people approving of the Act (Steinberg et al. 1997). Public support for active, voluntary euthanasia administered by doctors only for those suffering from terminal illness has increased dramatically over a 40-year period. In the period between 1947 and 1990, US public support for this form of euthanasia increased from two-thirds opposed to two-thirds in favour (Glick 1992, p. 84). Canadian public support is strong, with 76 per cent in favour in 1995 (Robinson 1998) and British figures also reflect continuing support over a number of years with 69 per cent of people in favour in 1976 (Williams 1989, p. 204) and 75 per cent in 1989 (Helme 1992, p. 71).

However, it is also widely acknowledged that most members of the public are unaware of the ethical dilemmas involved in assisting people to die. Surveys of doctors and nurses are therefore of particular interest. Much of the research addresses these issues in relation to the role of the doctor (Ashby & Wakefield 1993; Stevens & Hassan 1994; Komesaroff et al. 1995; Waddell et al. 1996; Kuhse et al. 1997; Baume 1998). The majority of doctors, it seems, support active voluntary euthanasia, but they are less supportive than the general community. It is worth noting the difficulty of comparing the results of the surveys, or of using them in some way as supportive of one argument, as their methodology differs—a factor which is not often acknowledged. The same methodological problems apply to surveys of nurses, who also appear to support active voluntary euthanasia (Stevens & Hassan 1994). Kitchener (1998) found that nurses are less in favour of active voluntary euthanasia than the public, but more in favour than medical practitioners. As doctors are the ones who would be called upon to assist in ending a terminally ill person's life, this finding reflects the weight of responsibility felt by those who dedicate their lives to the preservation of life. The finding also indicates that doctors are, to some extent, aware of the anticipated legal and ethical difficulties in actually assisting someone to die.

Research and comment on euthanasia and decision-making at the end of life point to many of the ethical, clinical and social dimensions which complicate the experience of terminal illness and the provision of appropriate care in the time before death (Slomka 1992; Kelner & Bourgeault 1993; Caddell & Newton 1995; Seale & Addington-Hall 1995; Guadagnoli & Ward 1998; Charles et al. 1999). While end-of-life decisions no doubt necessitate medical and ethical debate, they are also significant sociocultural issues which require socially oriented research. How, for instance, can personal attitudes to facing death be interpreted in terms of the social and historical processes taking place within modern Western societies? Two themes are evident within research ranging over a period of more than 40 years. The first is a move towards increasing personal involvement in decision-making at the end of life. This involvement reflects a concern to maintain control over projects of self-identity (Seale et al. 1997) and a focus upon individualism, but also a degree of public dissatisfaction with medicine. The second theme informs much of this dissatisfaction, as institutionalised and medicalised dying and death have become part of Western contemporary life (Blauner 1966). Medicalisation of dying and death has, until very recently, been accepted as 'normal'. Medical authority, together with the increasing use of life-supporting and life-prolonging technologies, have become part of a commonly held discourse of dying and death as I discuss in more detail in Chapter 6.

Division of opinion and practice exists in all areas of terminal care, and while euthanasia is certainly the most controversial of these, it is but one topic amidst an array of ethically charged concerns. High-technology intensive care facilities in major hospitals coexist with hospices and palliative care services, but our societies are yet to agree completely upon who should receive which kind of care and in what circumstances. The hospice and palliative care services have increased in number, but are still unevenly distributed and subject to stringent funding restrictions in many countries around the world. In view of these inconsistencies, many people within Western societies find that they have very little say in how their care will be organised in the last days of their lives.

MEDICAL MANAGEMENT IN THE LAST DAYS OF LIFE

Even though in the normal course of life we bracket off thoughts which threaten our existential security (Giddens 1991), we are occasionally called on to consider how we might face dying and death. Unless we are killed instantaneously by accident, it is likely that our dying will involve some kind of medical management. The increasing degree of medical authority invested in the management of dying has stimulated research in the area of living wills or advance directives for medical treatment of life-threatening, unacceptable and irreversible illness (Molloy & Guyatt 1991; Waddell et al. 1997). An advance directive is a document that allows people to plan their future health care. The directive helps to alleviate the difficult decisions that may fall to family, friends and doctors when, through age, illness or accident, people lose their capacity to make informed decisions about their treatment. In a survey I conducted with Charles Waddell (1997), we asked two groups of people to respond to a scenario in the manner of an advance directive. Answers from the Anglo Australian group gave us an indication of how people in the dominant cultural group within Australia think about facing death, while the Chinese Australian respondents' answers illustrated how, within a multicultural environment, people have quite different attitudes to facing death.

The two groups were asked the following question: 'If you had a life-threatening irreversible illness (that is, a disease or injury that would leave lasting disabilities which are unacceptable to you), and you were unable to give consent or communicate, how would you desire the doctors to treat you?' They were given a choice of fixed-response answers from which they could choose to be:

- admitted to an Intensive Care Unit (ICU) and have everything possible done to maintain life including ventilation;
- admitted to surgical care for intervention but not to the level of ICU;
- admitted to palliative care to be kept warm, dry, pain free and provided with sustenance, but without x-rays, blood tests or antibiotics;
- allowed to have a natural death with no medical or sustenance intervention, except pain relief; or
- allowed a medically assisted death (otherwise known as active euthanasia).

The degree to which the respondents agreed with advance directives was gauged by a question which asked them whether they would like to have their desired level of care documented so that doctors and their family would know what they wanted. The two groups were also asked: 'If a person has a life-threatening irreversible illness and wishes an assisted death, should that be available?'

The results of the survey illustrate that Anglo Australians (88 per cent) are more likely to favour advanced directives or living wills than Chinese Australians (71 per cent). It is interesting that, while both groups mostly favour advanced directives, many people do not actually go to the trouble of planning for future irreversible illnesses. In a Canadian survey, 10 per cent of the respondents reported they had completed a living will (Singer et al. 1995). Situational factors, such as organisational characteristics (Castle & Mor 1998) and unwillingness on the part of family members and doctors to acknowledge that the patient is hopelessly ill (Teno et al. 1998), further complicate the process of enacting advance directives when people are close to death. This kind of research demonstrates the contrast between people who respond to a seemingly straightforward question about how they wish to plan for future death with the actual circumstances of dying and witnessing death. A study by Winland-Brown (1998) of seventeen older persons described why they chose not to formalise their end-of-life decisions. This study reflects many of my own observations, finding that the participants in the research vacillated between fear and acceptance of death, trust and mistrust of others, and the assumption of immortality and the inevitability of death. The ambivalence associated with advance directives is also seen in survey responses regarding end-of-life care. In our survey, palliative care was favoured by 48 per cent of both Anglo and Chinese Australians, though more Chinese Australians would opt for ICU (33 per cent) than Anglo Australians (23 per cent). Directives for a medically assisted death differed also, with 18 per cent of the Chinese Australians and 30 per cent of the Anglo Australians suggesting they would prefer this option. Australian society is obviously diverse, though this has been demonstrated here by only one comparison, that of two ethnic groups. Yet there are many other factors which contribute to multiple moral traditions (Turner 1998) and sociocultural circumstances, all of which challenge a common morality and a common way to approach death.

Euthanasia is the most controversial of the issues surrounding death in contemporary times. When asked a general question about belief in active euthanasia, 68 per cent of Anglo Australians and 51 per cent of Chinese Australians agreed that euthanasia should be available for those who wish to take this option. Clearly there is a division within both ethnic groups, a factor which makes it difficult to determine exactly what affects people's beliefs. Caddell and Newton (1995) found that highly educated, politically liberal respondents with a less religious self-perception are most likely to accept active euthanasia. Yet religious belief is more complex than it first appears, as a study by Hamil-Luker and Smith (1998) demonstrates. They have shown that, in some traditions, people's euthanasia attitudes are not congruent with the positions of their religious authorities, though in other traditions—most notably evangelicalism—religious authority appears to remain strong. If we can accept that nurses share a similar level of education, we see the division within this group, with 66 per cent of nurses willing to be involved in the procedure providing it were legal (Kitchener 1998). Nurses, of course, have a far more detailed knowledge of the circumstances of euthanasia, but still we see a division within the group regarding a belief in active voluntary euthanasia. MacDonald (1998) conducted a study to see how attitudes towards voluntary euthanasia vary across different categories (the type of assistance, the type of illness and the age of the patient). It appears people differ in their attitudes to the availability of voluntary euthanasia according to whether the patient has cancer or Alzheimer's disease, with the cancer patients' requests receiving more support. MacDonald suggests that the findings of the study reflect a concern about safeguarding the patients' autonomy in the decision-making process. Perhaps this latter finding is more crucial than studies that try to identify variables determining belief in active voluntary euthanasia. Authority of the individual is of particular importance, but still we have two groups: those who agree that this authority should extend to assistance in dying and those who do not.

EUTHANASIA AND TERMINAL ILLNESS

Euthanasia is an issue which seems to divide communities, but the question of whether one would wish for personal euthanasia is complex. One of the interesting findings of our survey is that people are more likely to agree with the principle of euthanasia than to envisage themselves asking for assistance in ending their own lives (30 per cent of Anglo Australians and 18 per cent of Chinese Australians). When people are terminally ill, the issue of euthanasia becomes even more complicated. Occasionally there are people who consistently ask for euthanasia and are very sure of their decision, though many medical professionals debate whether depression or social isolation contributes to these requests (Kissane et al. 1998). Not all people who request euthanasia are depressed or socially isolated, though obviously these are issues which need to be considered when listening to those who wish to die. I was present with Matthew, a resident hospice doctor, when Irene spoke extensively about her wish to receive euthanasia. Irene was in her early seventies, with few family members. She had never married and did not have children. A professional woman all her life, she was used to controlling her own life, was fiercely independent and strongly resented having to rely on other people to do everything for her. She expressed a strong wish to end her life, saying that she felt happy with the way her life had unfolded until she found that her disease had incapacitated her completely. Irene felt she had little more to achieve and, believing that her life lacked dignity, thought that it was her right to end her life with medical assistance. An intelligent woman, Irene presented her case with insight, anticipating and arguing against the counter-arguments she was well aware she would encounter.

Irene expressed an overwhelming lethargy unlike anything she had ever experienced in her life, and while she repeatedly requested euthanasia for a period of time, she gradually became weaker and withdrew from social interaction. She told me she was angry and when she heard that I was a social scientist she said that I should do something to change what she believed was an 'appalling injustice'. Matthew listened patiently, but acknowledged to her that he was powerless to help. The remainder of the hospice staff demonstrated mixed reactions; some simply ignored Irene's requests and on one occasion I heard two nurses and a doctor making remarks about how they should put Irene in the room across from another patient who had made similar requests. 'Then at least they could talk to one another, because there is nothing that we can do,' one of the nurses remarked. Irene did not appear depressed when we spoke with her and Matthew did not consider her to be clinically depressed. Whether she gradually became depressed while waiting to die, or simply withdrew in the manner of many dying people who begin their social death before their bodies give way, is open to dispute. Another patient, Salvatore, also asked for euthanasia and became quite angry when he was denied medical assistance to end his life. Like Irene, Salvatore never had close family; however, it is debatable whether they should be classified as 'socially isolated'—both had many friends and had experienced full and satisfying work lives. Having spent three hours listening to Salvatore's stories of life and dying, I did not think him depressed or withdrawn.

I once accompanied Patrick, a very experienced and well-respected palliative care doctor, while we visited Louis, a charming retired judge who was suffering from colon cancer and had been admitted to the hospice for respite. Louis walked down the corridor of the hospice in purple silk pyjamas and a matching red and purple spotted gown. He shook our hands, conducted us to seats in his room, but did not sit down himself. Over the course of an hour and a half, the three of us discussed the options Louis had for the remaining course of his life, though Patrick and I mostly listened. Louis had a personal story which was punctuated by great tragedy, and he had many issues left to resolve with his family. Louis was unsure whether he wanted to attempt to resolve these issues, as he felt this may not be possible: it may cause more harm than good, and he was not entirely sure that he wanted to invest the emotional energy in such a project. He had two families, one with his first wife who had suicided and a second which was a happier and closer knit group. Louis paced the floor, first giving one argument and then the counter in true legal fashion, while Patrick nodded sympathetically and continued to propose further curative treatment so that Louis could extend his life in order to address unresolved issues with his first family. Patrick carefully avoided discussion relating to euthanasia which Louis introduced on three occasions. However, in reality, the choice to receive medical assistance to end his life was hypothetical, and although he received a sympathetic ear, palliative care practitioners are for the most part very outspoken in their opposition to euthanasia, as I discuss in Chapter 8.

Hypothetically, all three of the people I have discussed could be candidates for euthanasia. None was in severe physical pain, they appeared rational, and put forward good arguments in support of having assistance to end their lives. However, in Louis' case he was capable of living for some time and could have further quality of life. Other terminally ill people have a far harder journey through terminal illness. I discussed one of the patients who received assistance to end their lives under the Northern Territory *Rights of the Terminally Ill Act* with two senior palliative care practitioners. Though both were publicly outspoken in their opposition to euthanasia, they both also agreed that Mrs Janet Mills, the second person to take advantage of the Act, was a patient who was a 'good candidate for euthanasia'. Mrs Mills had a rare form of skin cancer which caused intractable pain. Even the latest advances in palliative medicine could not help Mrs Mills who, in her own words, achieved 'peace at last' in death. There are other people who could be helped by being assisted to die, but the health professionals who are called upon to assist are burdened by the enormous task of determining the ethical, legal and social issues involved in every case. In Chapter 8 I discuss the extended case history of a woman called Marnie who did not have her request for euthanasia honoured but spent her last days unconscious through medical sedation. The story of Marnie highlights the difficulty of decision-making when the ravages of disease and the tragedy of life's events rob a person of the ability to make rational decisions. Even when health professionals can, in all good conscience, make a decision based on 'rights to life' or 'rights to death' morality, they are burdened by clinical and social uncertainties.

DO TERMINALLY ILL PEOPLE SPEAK ABOUT DYING?

Many terminally ill people *do* want to die, but not all ask for assistance to end their lives. Seale and Addington-Hall (1994) analysed the results of two surveys in England of relatives and others who knew people who had died in the years 1987 and 1990. Of those who expressed a view about the subject, about a quarter of both the respondents and the people who died preferred an earlier death. In the 1990 study, 3.6 per cent reported that euthanasia had been requested at some time during the last year of the terminally ill person's life. It is interesting that this study found that social class and religious faith were largely insignificant in influencing feelings of wanting to die earlier and requests for euthanasia. Dependency was, however, very important in both wanting to die earlier and asking for help in ending life. These results confirm observations about the importance of individualism and autonomy in Western societies. McInerney (2000) argues that 'requested death' is a new social movement involving the reclamation of matters of identity, privacy and individuality. In another paper based on the same surveys mentioned above, Seale and Addington-Hall (1995) propose that the wish for euthanasia is more an assertion of personal control than an act of surrender. They found that people who had received hospice care were more likely to have wished to die earlier. However, they suggest that this finding must be understood in the light of palliative care practices which encourage patients to express their fears and wishes. All too often we have no idea of how terminally ill people think and feel because, as Elias (1985) writes in his book *The Loneliness of Dying*, most people are lost for words and are overwhelmed with embarrassment when visiting terminally ill people. Even many health professionals avoid personal communications with dying people and often patient expectations for good patient–health professional communication are not met (Kutner et al. 1999).

In my discussions with terminally ill people, I took the lead from the many skilled and empathetic palliative care practitioners I observed. These practitioners patiently wait for the terminally ill person or their close family member to introduce the topic of dying. Palliative care practitioners speak of waiting for 'permission' to discuss dying and death. The permission may be given immediately and spontaneously, not at all or after some kind of trust has been established. I spoke with many hospice staff about Georgie, a patient who spent several weeks at the hospice. At 44 years of age, Georgie developed cancer which spread to her spine, leaving her paralysed from her waist down. Until the very last days of her life, Georgie, and to some extent, her professional carers, seemed totally absorbed with Georgie's problem with her paralysis and her bowel management. Discussion with Georgie and about Georgie related mostly to physical symptoms like pain control, and particularly to what kind of bowel treatments she was receiving for constipation. Felicity, the social worker, told me that Georgie was using the 'obsession with the constipation' as a way of avoiding speaking about death, but Pat, the physiotherapist, said that Georgie knew 'what was going on . . . she just didn't want to talk about it'. It was hard to know what Georgie thought because she did not articulate her beliefs about what she thought would happen to her in the future—her concern was for the present. Some time after Georgie's death I interviewed Pat, who told me she had many talks with Georgie about dying. Pat knew that she alone was the one person Georgie had confided in. 'We had so much in common,' Pat suggested. 'We were the same age, had similar interests . . . it was hard to watch her die.'

Some families will never discuss the approaching death of a loved one and the silence weighs heavy as that person deteriorates and finally passes away. These patients are the 'silent terminals'—discussion about death is avoided and the patients and families use silence as a coping mechanism. I discuss truth-telling and open discussion about death more fully in Chapter 7, but it is worth noting here the ground-breaking research by Glaser and Strauss (1966, 1968), who explored the dying trajectories of terminally ill cancer patients. They saw that dying is a time where terminally ill people undergo a series of changes which signal a role shift from socially productive to socially non-productive members of society. The experience of each terminally ill person is dependent to some extent upon the resolution of uncertainties, but this resolution is closely linked to the nature of communication between professional hospital staff, patients and their families. Glaser and Strauss (1966) identify four kinds of communication patterns between the staff and patients and their families which they refer to as *awareness contexts*.

The *closed awareness context* arose when the staff (and to some extent the patient's family) knew the terminal prognosis but the patient did not. *Suspicion awareness* was where the staff and family knew and the patient suspected and often used strategies to elicit information from caregivers to find out the truth. *Mutual pretence* was when all parties concerned knew of the terminal prognosis but did not acknowledge it. In the *open awareness* scenario, the terminal prognosis was known to the patient, the family members and the staff. All of those concerned were able to talk about the prognosis openly and to discuss its consequences. It appeared that the closed awareness context was most likely to break down into other types of communication contexts over time. In contrast to the high prevalence of closed awareness at the time that Glaser and Strauss did their research, some research suggests that people are now more likely to adopt open awareness strategies (Seale et al. 1997). Seale and colleagues found that those adopting a position of open awareness, as opposed to a closed awareness position, were more likely to have cancer, not be mentally confused, and be in a higher social class. These groups of people are more able to plan their dying careers, are less likely to die alone and have more choice, particularly in relation to where they die. The most recent discussion of awareness contexts (Field & Copp 1999) reviews an array of death-related research and suggests that many terminally ill people and their professional carers engage in a form of conditional awareness. Awareness is therefore dependent on a number of factors which change over time, and the context of each situation is all important.

CONCLUSION

People do think and talk about facing death, though this is obviously not a popular topic. Thoughts and discussions about death are not taboo, but they are awkward, and we invariably tend to hesitate before engaging in lengthy discussions on the topic. Has the person we are talking to lost a loved one? Have they ever had a cancer diagnosis? What are their opinions about euthanasia? Do they believe in life after death? All of these questions temper the tone of the conversation. So can one become accustomed to the idea of facing death? I have found that nurses who work in palliative care agree that you can get used to the idea of death, and some nurses even admitted to an 'almost light-hearted' response to death. Louise said: 'I've learnt that death can indeed be peaceful as opposed to violent.' Nevertheless, these comments are in some ways removed from the extremely personal response one has when facing his or her own death. Another nurse, Angela, told me how, after suffering a stroke at an unusually young age, she was better able to understand the frightening reality of dying. Janice, who had a melanoma removed the year before she started palliative care nursing, said:

> When you actually look death in the face you can't resolve it—it is only at such a time when there is an individual response to the possibility of dying that you realise what it is about and you think it must be also about living life to the optimum—all the same it scares you.

Death can be frightening; even facing the death of other people on a daily basis can eventually take its toll. The words of Margaret, a nurse who had burned out from caring for dying people, illustrate the enormous weight associated with death work:

> I literally burned out . . . I became revolted by death. I remember a patient lying in a small dark room and he was dirty. I had to touch him and wash him . . . I had such an awful revulsion and he was gasping his last breath. I had always coped before, I felt I let myself down. Will someone turn away from me when I am dying?

Will someone turn away from us when we are dying? For we will all die despite our diet and exercise regimes and all of the marvels of modern medicine?

This chapter has demonstrated that people do think about facing death but, as Giddens (1991) argues, in the normal course of life we bracket off thoughts about our own deaths. We need not agree with Gorer (1965) that this reluctance to talk about death is pathological or 'pornographic', but we can see, as Giddens suggests, that neglecting death is indeed part of building a functioning society unperturbed by the reality of chaos. Nevertheless, when death does come, our world-view changes and we must draw upon our resources to face the chaos. I have reviewed some of the literature about people's attitudes to facing death, particularly in relation to advanced directives and euthanasia, and I have contributed aspects from my own research. One theme is particularly evident: people may change their opinions about dying when they are faced with death themselves. We can so easily formulate hypothetical theories, but our own dying no doubt will be overlayed with anxiety and uncertainty. We have also seen, importantly, that those who feel able to discuss their own or their loved one's approaching death are more likely to have the control so highly valued in contemporary Western societies. Nevertheless, there are limits to this control, and we are all, as members of society, subject to the regulations of the state which forbid euthanasia. Individual autonomy has limits and we, as members of liberal societies, continue to debate the boundaries of these limits in our discussions of 'rights to life' and 'rights to death'.

three

The cancer story

For many people, a cancer diagnosis is a death warrant. Cancer occupies such an insidious place in the public imagination that the association between cancer and death is now well entrenched in popular myth. Kellehear (1990, p. 65) suggests that if you have a malignant cancer, both 'popular and professional views often define you as dying'. This chapter attempts to investigate why, despite encouraging trends in the reduction in mortality in some cancers, the association between cancer and death continues. It is no wonder that misinformation and fear about cancer take root in contemporary Western societies as there are a multiplicity of messages about the disease which inevitably create uncertainty. These messages are presented in professional and lay discourse. They come from the scientific community, from general practitioners and specialist doctors, from the vast array of alternative practitioners, from the media, from public health and from our neighbours, work colleagues and families. We are told of the hope that exists in new cures and therapies and of the drawn-out deaths of those who have 'lost the battle' against the dreaded disease. Messages of hope and despair combine, fuelling a cultural terror and exposing our inherent fragility, our fear of death.

No one is more fragile than the cancer sufferer. How is dying from cancer different then from dying from an accident, from a heart attack or from 'old age'? It is particularly important that we understand these distinctions because the cancer sufferer is burdened by the stigma which gives cancer a symbolic life of its own (Sontag 1978). The newly diagnosed cancer patient is debilitated not only by the *symptoms* of the disease, but also by the *symbols* of the disease. Cancer is associated with pollution, with uncontrollable and overwhelming growth, and with evil. It is—and has been for some time now—a derogatory word, unlike stroke or Parkinson's disease which are more likely to evoke sympathy rather than fear. It is not that we are unsympathetic to the cancer sufferer, it is that cancer has a life beyond the particular disease that changes a family member's or friend's life forever. It is important to understand the life beyond the disease because cancer is very much a part of our lived experiences and our world-views. Malignant neoplasms are now the leading cause of death in many countries around the world, including Australia, the United Kingdom and the United States (World Health Organisation 1996). The risk of developing cancer is high with one in three men and one in four women being directly affected by cancer in their lifetime (Australian Bureau of Statistics 2000).

CANCER AND DEATH IN CONTEMPORARY TIMES

Cancer is an epidemiologically complex problem which is present in all parts of the world. A worldwide estimate for annual mortality from all cancer and for 25 specific cancer sites around 1990 shows that, of the 5.2 million deaths from cancer, 55 per cent occurred in developing countries (Pisani et al. 1999). However, deaths from cancer also continue in developed countries and recent studies which emphasise the decline in cancer mortality (Levi et al. 1999; Wingo et al. 1998) fail to note the much sharper decline in heart disease mortality (Clapp 1998). Success in reducing mortality is encouraging, particularly the recent trend in survival of people aged under 35 diagnosed with leukaemia, Hodgkin's disease and testicular cancer (Reeves et al. 1999). Understandably, the apparent successes warrant increased preventive cancer control efforts, as cancer poses a particularly heavy burden on individuals and communities alike. Nevertheless, attention must also be given to those who are dying of cancer, for there are huge emotional and financial burdens associated with end-of-life care. A recent study (Weeks et al. 1998) confirmed previous findings that cancer patients tend to overestimate the probability of long-term survival and that these estimates may influence their preferences about medical therapies. Vigano and colleagues (1999) found that doctors also appear to overestimate the duration of life of terminally ill cancer patients. This has prompted them to suggest that clinical estimation of survival should be considered as just one criterion, rather than as the sole determinant in providing adequate end-of-life care.

Levin (1999, p. 105) asks whether cancer is 'the pestilence of our time'. He suggests that cancer cannot simply be attributed to the longevity of modern populations, as it strikes both young and old alike. Drawing upon the work of the influential theorist Michel Foucault, Levin proposes that part of what drives the many misconceptions and 'collective terror' about cancer is that we sense cancer's timeliness. It takes on what Foucault has called an historical individuality: 'cancer is THE illness of our time' (Herzlich & Pierret 1987, p. 55). We could argue that AIDS has replaced cancer in this respect, but for most people in Western societies AIDS is a disease which affects marginal populations of drug users and homosexual men. Cancer, by way of contrast, typifies our postmodern societies, for cancer stories come from young and old, male and female, rich and poor, and from the margins and mainstream of the societies we live in. Gordon (1990, p. 292) proposes that cancer is referred to as the 'illness of modern civilisation' because of the toxicity of our physical and mental environments. This toxicity feeds cancer so that it has the power to defy modern medicine's efforts to control decay, suffering and ultimately death.

Cancer has become the metaphor for the feared death. Different diseases are thought to assume a symbolic life of their own and this can vary in different times and places (Sontag 1978, 1989). Sontag has illustrated how cancer is closely associated with death in much the same way as leprosy and tuberculosis were in Victorian England. It is the multi-determined—and therefore mysterious—nature of cancer that Sontag suggests prompts metaphoric associations. While medicine continues to search for cures and therapies, it cannot combat the metaphoric associations, for cancer is thought to be socially and morally wrong. Undoubtedly medicine has contributed significantly to the continuing control of cancer. 'Age-standardised cancer incidence has actually been falling in both men and women since the early 1990s, and mortality rates have been falling in men since the mid-1980s and in women for most of the century' (Coates 1998, p. 8). Nuland (1993, p. 220) writes that, in 1930, 'only one in five people with cancer survived five years'. By the 1960s, biomedical research started to come to the fore and the number of 'survivors' reached one in three. Australian data reflects trends identified in countries with similar cancer profiles, including the United Kingdom and the United States, with approximately 50 per cent of people diagnosed with cancer now surviving beyond five years (Australian Bureau of Statistics 2000).

Despite these encouraging statistics, cancer is frightening to us all. Nuland (1993, p. 207) uses evocative language to describe cancer. 'Its cells behave like the members of a barbarian horde run amok—leaderless and undirected, but with a single-minded purpose: to plunder everything in its reach.' He goes on to demonstrate why cancer is thought of as an uncontrollable growth:

> Cancer cells cultivated in the laboratory exhibit an unlimited capacity to grow and generate new tumours . . . The combination of delayed death and uncontrolled birth are malignancy's greatest violation of the natural order of things. These two factors in combination are the main reasons a cancer, unlike normal tissue, continues to enlarge throughout its lifetime (1993, p. 210).

Nuland, a physician, presents us with two kinds of messages: one of hope in the survival rates, and another of fear in the descriptions of cancer's capacity for uncontrollable growth. Messages of hope and fear about cancer are often mixed, and people tend to focus on the bad news and the fear rather than the positive advances in cancer control. In the late twentieth century, the positive result of a biopsy replaced the Grim Reaper as the most potent symbol of death (Lupton 1994, p. 44). As Stacey (1997, p. 73) notes, following a cancer diagnosis death becomes life's only certainty and we can no longer pretend immortality through health and fitness and workaholism.

WHY IS CANCER THE FEARED DEATH?

There are several reasons why dying from cancer is feared, the foremost of which is the lack of knowledge about cancer causation. As Sontag (1978) has noted, the nature of cancer's causality is multifaceted. Despite a search for the aetiology of cancer which has a 4000-year history (Wolff 1989), at the beginning of a new millennium the quest continues. Medicine has of late moved away from 'the language of first causes' towards 'concepts of dynamically interactive fields' borrowed from the disciplines of physics, chemistry and biology (Levin 1999, p. 108). However, these moves do not yet embrace the totality of the cancer experience. Despite contemporary shifts in disease models, biomedicine still fails to account for the emotional, social, cultural and spiritual complexity of cancer. Clinical studies have indicated connections between chronic stress and cancer and between relationship losses and cancer onset (Pearce & Findlay 1987; Selye 1986). Nevertheless, findings which propose emotional, psychological and social factors as significant causes of cancer are still highly contentious (Lowenthal 1989). The alternative health movement has, in many ways, stimulated an interest in the non-physical causative agents. Variation in beliefs about cancer causation, however, do not fit into a neat dichotomy with the biomedical explanations opposing 'alternative' explanations. Cultural interpretations of cancer are derived from a complex interplay 'between bodily processes and cultural categories' (Kleinman 1988, p. 14) and both biomedicine and alternative healing are culturally grounded, one in the culture of science and the other in the culture of non-science. The continuing controversy and uncertainty over cancer heighten the fear associated with the disease and with the cancer death.

Field (1996, p. 256) suggests that cancer is associated with the 'feared' death because of a number of factors. First, cancer is feared because it typically appears unexpectedly. Although it is not unusual for cancer sufferers to interpret their cancer as a warning to review and change their lifestyles (Dodds 1997), this understanding is constructed in retrospect and it is unlikely that many people expect to get cancer. Field explains that cancer is also untimely, affecting very young people as well as middle-aged and older adults. In contemporary society, death normally comes after a reasonably long life. Where in earlier generations death may have been a constant threat, in our situation 'death before the due time is all the more difficult to deal with' (Ballard 1996, p. 9). Field also proposes that there is a fair degree of certainty concerning the terminal prognosis, although—as I have already noted—research shows that cancer patients and their doctors tend to overestimate the length of time they will live. Lastly, Field notes that the nature of dying is often painful and prolonged. Modern palliative care has controlled much of the pain and suffering associated with dying from cancer, though not every cancer sufferer receives good palliative care. A recent British study (Addington-Hall et al. 1998) which sought to investigate which terminally ill cancer patients receive palliative care found that admission to hospices and specialist palliative care units was governed more by chance than need. Additionally, many people do not know what palliative care is—a survey conducted by Palliative Care Australia indicated half of the community have no knowledge of palliative care (Medicus 1999). Lack of consistent quality care at the end of life and lack of knowledge contribute to the fear associated with the cancer death.

Cancer is highly stigmatised and this complicates the fear associated with the disease. Historically, cancer has been linked with contagion, a notion that seemed to go in and out of favour right through to the turn of the twentieth century (Cassileth 1983). Sontag (1978, p. 43) argues that the ancient Greeks believed the disease to be the result of either supernatural punishment, demonic possession or the result of natural causes. However, stigmatisation did not just occur in ancient and more recent modern history: it is also a very real problem for cancer sufferers in contemporary times. Pinell (1987) analysed letters written by cancer patients who contributed to a French public debate on cancer. One patient wrote: 'Friends avoid you, not knowing what to say, and it's a mistake, one should speak about it; it is less frightening' (1987, p. 36). Other research (Balshem 1991) identified a fatalism in working-class

Americans which was entrenched in 'an integrated structure of belief about the essential nature of cancer' (1991, p. 161):

> As with most minions of fate, cancer may punish those who notice or defy it. To think about cancer, to try to prevent it, is to tempt fate. Cancer testing is 'looking for trouble'. Respondents seemed hesitant to speak the word 'cancer' out loud, and they often referred to cancer as 'the big C'.

Fatalism is only part of a much more complex picture of blame and responsibility associated with cancer. Other members of the public may be more receptive to recent health promotion messages prominent within the new public health movement (Petersen & Lupton 1996), which imbue the cancer diagnosis with additional cultural meaning.

We now know that the majority of cancers are due to environmental and lifestyle factors such as tobacco and alcohol consumption, nutritional deficiencies or excesses, reproductive and sexual behaviour, pollution and occupation (New South Wales Cancer Council 1996). Worldwide data indicate that 20 per cent of all cancer deaths could be prevented by eliminating smoking, and that infectious agents account for a further 16 per cent (Pisani et al. 1999). This kind of evidence tends to shift the blame for the disease from some unknown agent or agents to the sufferer. Fear of the cancer death can in some ways be complicated by the guilt we may feel when engaging in so called 'risky' behaviours. Public health discourse emphasises a moral and cultural climate that focuses on individual responsibility for health and welfare. The public health discourse is one of the many explanatory models (Kleinman 1980) which further complicate the messages the public hears about cancer. Whether we are fatalistic or vigilant in our monitoring of cancer risks, whether we favour reductionist biomedical explanations or psychologically based explanations like the 'typical' cancer personality (Le Shan 1977; Chen et al. 1995), we still cannot seem to escape the association between cancer and death. They are an unfortunate pair and the myth continues despite advances in cancer control and the hope that exists in the hearts of so many cancer sufferers. As Pinell (1987, p. 27) observes, cancer is portrayed as a challenge to rationality—it seems as if cancer is an outcome of a kind of social and bodily disorder which brings about death.

THE FRAGILE LIVES OF CANCER SUFFERERS

In order to understand how people die of cancer, we must understand the illness experience and the dying trajectory (Glaser & Strauss 1966). Cancer changes the sufferer's life forever, for even if that person is able to go on living, he or she lives under threat of possible recurrence of the disease. The diagnosis of cancer constitutes a major existential threat and sufferers are prompted to reevaluate their lives and dreams. Kellehear (1996, p. 157) notes that 'in the period during and after the crisis, one's whole way of understanding life may need revision because a major part is found wanting. The meaning and value of one's life may be called into question.' This questioning becomes part of a new cancer identity whereby the sufferer tries to make sense not just of his or her illness, but also of life (Mathieson & Stam 1995, p. 284). Cancer patients suffer a great weight of responsibility for they are expected to take up the fight against the dreaded disease and this becomes not just their own personal battle, but a part of a far greater story:

> Cancer patients stand accused primarily of a failure of will. Small wonder they have been shunned and shamed in our recent history, hidden like a consummate obscenity from public view . . . In the new age of consumption driven postmodern enlightenment we are more inclined to rehabilitate cancer patients than punish them, less inclined to isolate and destroy. So today we cajole. We infuse cancer with the power of good thoughts, optimism, and above all will power! (Levin 1999, p. 106)

It seems that hope and the will to fight are not simply options for cancer sufferers but expectations placed upon them by family, friends, health professionals and indeed the broader society.

Lupton (1994, p. 67) notes that hope is prominent in approaches to cancer in Western societies. She explains that the military and invasion metaphors common to frightening diseases like cancer are used to convince cancer patients that they must 'win' by adopting a positive attitude. 'To despair, to lose hope, are frowned upon as strategies of dealing with diseases such as cancer.' Walder (1994, p. 67), who writes of her own experience of breast cancer, explains that she was influenced by suggestions that a positive mental attitude would help her control a recurrence of the disease. However, describing herself as 'a worrier', she was concerned that her own personality would limit her capacity to transform the disease. In their struggles to overcome cancer, patients turn to a variety of services, including those offered through conventional and alternative medicine. Many patients with metastatic cancer (secondary involvement) choose alternative therapies in their attempts to overcome terminal cancer. Forty per cent of the sample in one study reported using some kind of alternative therapy and 21 per cent said they adhered to an alternative treatment regimen (Yates et al. 1993). By the time most cancer patients reach the terminal phase of their illness, they have followed a complicated path which has taken them through various treatments, some invasive and costly and some less so. The experience is characterised as an ordeal which is heavily medicalised and stigmatised to such an extent that many cancer patients do not access community services and networks that may assist them (Muzzin et al. 1994). Costain Schou and Hewison (1999, pp. 24–5) also suggest that health professionals often minimise the seriousness of cancer and its treatment, thereby focusing on the cognitive-behavioural responses of patients rather than the social, political and ethical issues embedded in the context of diagnosis and treatments.

Hope is an important component both in the fight against cancer and in coping with a terminal illness (Perakyla 1991). However, another theme which dominates the cancer sufferer's life is that of uncertainty. The existential, social, clinical and moral uncertainties surrounding dying and death are recurring themes throughout this book and they reappear here in the cancer story. Uncertainty surrounds the cancer illness and trajectory and this uncertainty does not relate just to death but to issues of pain, dependency, loneliness and life themes (Zlatin 1995). Little and colleagues (1998) use the term 'liminality' to explain the experiences of patients suffering from cancer of the colon. The liminal phase is a period of time beginning with the first manifestations of malignancy which is marked by feelings of disorientation, a sense of loss and of loss of control, and uncertainty. Gradually each patient begins to construct and reconstruct meaning based on their own experiences which are grounded in the changing of the body and the self. Many of these changing experiences are overlayed by a persistent identification as a cancer patient, regardless of the time since the treatment and the presence or absence of persistent or recurrent disease. There is also a persistent sense of boundedness which makes each person supremely aware of limits to space, empowerment and available time.

DYING OF CANCER

The outdated, though influential, work of Kubler-Ross (1969) outlines a five-stage model of dying, proposing that dying patients (most notably those dying from cancer) go through a process of denial, anger, bargaining, depression and acceptance. While Kubler-Ross's work tends to ignore the context of each case (Charmaz 1980) it did draw much needed attention to the lives and suffering of terminally ill people who, in the pre-hospice era, were often relegated to large impersonal hospital wards and treated as socially dead before their actual demise (Sudnow 1967). Research like that of Little et al. (1998), discussed above, is far more open-ended, as indeed are the lives of cancer sufferers who may recover from their disease or follow the tragic course of terminal illness and eventual death. For those cancer patients who enter the terminal stage of their illness, their lives will become part of what I call a living dying.

At this stage, the cancer identity is more heavily imbued with failure. It is a spoiled identity (Goffman 1963) and is associated with decay, dirt, pain and death. The cancer sufferer completely loses the healthy image of the self which has in the past helped them to express similarity and solidarity with other people. During this time cancer patients enter a phase of enormous social and physical restriction.

Fear of loss of control, particularly over bodily functions, becomes of prime importance, as it does to other people who suffer from chronic disabling illnesses (Seymour 1998). Disabling symptoms force cancer patients to reassess their abilities to act as competent social agents and they may be forced to relinquish control to others. DiGiacomo (1987, p. 316), an anthropologist who was diagnosed with Hodgkin's disease, a cancer of the lymphatic system, adopted a strong attitude to identity as a way of managing her fear:

> In the hospital, my identity was assailed. It is difficult to be anything but what a total institution makes of you, and it is doubly difficult when the heavy symbolic charge of cancer is added to institutional require-ments . . . Identity, however, seemed to be the one area in which I could retain some control. I certainly could not control my body; that was now in the hands of my doctors.

A study which looked at cancer patients' reported experiences of suffering found that the primary sources of physical suffering were fatigue, pain and the side-effects of chemotherapy. Psychological suffering, most typically manifested in depression, and general deterioration and fear of infections also severely restricted the social life of the patients with incurable cancer (Kuuppelomaki & Lauri 1998). Dying of cancer is a complex matter and the pre-death experience of the cancer patient is subject to contradictions and chaos. There are no smooth pre-established and foolproof patterns in decision-making, acceptance of death or symp-tom control, as I demonstrate in the many case histories I discuss throughout this book.

When a person realises that they are dying of cancer, their greatest fears are realised. Fear—like hope and uncertainty—is an emotion common to the cancer patient and at some point they inevitably realise the true root of this fear. Of course, as I demonstrate in the stories of cancer patients I discuss elsewhere in the book, many people do not articulate this understanding, though others do talk about dying. Some people also begin preparations for dying. Kellehear (1990) interviewed 100 cancer patients who had been given a terminal prognosis and identified five key features in their preparations for death. He proposes that awareness of dying, social adjustments and personal preparations, public preparations, arrangements relating to work and farewells are ways in which people prepare to leave their families and friends. Preparations for funerals and the making of wills are ways in which we, as a society, acknowledge that death does happen. Field (1996, p. 256) argues that people are far more likely to have been informed that they are dying if they have terminal cancer. The kinds of uncertainties associated with determining a prognosis 'are more readily resolved for cancer deaths than for other terminal conditions'. The cancer death is different, then, from other kinds of dying. Cancer is generally not sudden and many people may have months, if not years, in which to contemplate their future death. However, despite the degree of comparative clinical certainty proposed by Field, huge gulfs of uncertainty exist for cancer patients. Certainty about death may grow, but uncertainty about managing pain, grief and loneliness may also continue.

A CANCER STORY

Narrative analysis is a well established way of understanding the illness experience, and this has been used to examine the subjective experience of cancer sufferers (Little et al. 1998). Through following the illness stories of patients, we are made aware of the common experiences of cancer sufferers—their pain, confusion and fear of death. Many of the broader themes I have identified in the research above are evident within the following account of my father's illness and death. When Dad received his cancer diagnosis, he had only recently retired after working until the obligatory retirement age of 65 years. Ignoring his few small 'bladder problems', it was some time before he suspected his symptoms indicated more than 'old age'. After initial tests, his general practitioner referred him to an oncologist who diagnosed Dad with a particularly aggressive prostate cancer. Mum described how the initial news was made more traumatic by the callous manner in which the doctor spoke about the diagnosis and prognosis. The oncologist accepted several telephone calls throughout the consultation and appeared very 'matter of fact'. This short moment was replayed in family conversations over a number of months and it came to take on a significance which complicated the trust so essential to good patient–doctor interaction. Dad underwent surgery and radiotherapy and kept up his visits to his general practitioner. Never one to engage in open discussions, he kept his fear and uncertainty to himself and attempted, like the participants in an American study (Muzzin et al. 1994), to maintain control and normalise everyday activity. It was difficult to make plans for the future, but Mum and Dad managed to have an overseas trip while Dad was relatively well.

Gradually, Dad's health deteriorated and he began to need help to get out of bed and make his routine visits to a medical doctor who was offering a controversial form of radiotherapy. Now, over ten years later,

I recall with sorrow how Dad, a very tall man, collapsed on top of me in the carpark after one of these visits. He was mortified and terribly concerned that he had hurt me. I could not lift him and we turned to strangers to help us. Despite his deterioration, Dad maintained hope that the therapy would either cure him, or at the very least keep him alive for a longer time. I have noticed that it is not unusual for patients to express 'unrealistic' hopes for the future and to continue both medical and alternative therapies in the hope of an extended life. This is not entirely their own doing, as medical practitioners are often implicated in the projection of hope through the uncertain nature of cancer therapies which include both successes and failures.

> The boundaries of medical futility, however, have never been clear and it may be too much to expect that they ever will be. It is perhaps for this reason that there has arisen the conviction among doctors—more than a mere conviction, it is nowadays felt by many to be a responsi-bility—that should error occur in the treatment of a patient, it must always be on the side of doing more rather than less (Nuland 1993, p. 221).

Dad's doctors adhered to this philosophy and, with his eager permission, he continued to receive aggressive therapy in combating his cancer until two weeks before his death. At that time, he lay in a large ward of a major hospital, his mouth sore from thrush and his weary and painful body wasting away. On hearing about palliative care through a friend, we then insisted that Dad be transferred to a palliative care unit where his symptoms were partially alleviated. I am sure palliative care is far better accepted now, but I am still surprised that not one of Dad's doctors suggested it. Although he never spoke of dying, Dad called for the Catholic priest to help him renew his long-lapsed faith. The night before he died, he fell when trying to get out of bed. The pain from his dislocated shoulder prompted the doctors to increase his dosage of morphine and Dad remained sedated until he died. This story is not dramatic, although it was—and still is—wounding to my family and to me. It is a common story; my father could be your father, husband, brother, neighbour or friend.

CONCLUSION

It is not surprising that the cancer death has been linked so closely with the euthanasia debate. Cancer is a complex phenomenon which I have argued has a life beyond the individual experience of suffering and death. The cultural meaning associated with cancer goes beyond that of other diseases which kill—stroke and heart disease evoke a clinical and symbolically sterile picture, whereas lung cancer brings to mind filthy tar-sodden lungs, hacking coughs, a growth beyond control. The cancer takes over individual identity so that the patient is no longer a person but a disease.

> The investigation required me to enter the hospital. Fluids were extracted, specialists' opinions accumulated, machines produced images of the insides of my body, but the diagnosis remained uncertain. One day I returned to my room and found a new sign below my name on the door. It said 'Lymphoma', a form of cancer I was suspected of having . . . my name had not been changed, it had been defined. 'Lymphoma' was a medical flag, planted as a claim on the territory of my body (Frank 1999, p. 221).

Frank, a social scientist, is able to describe the assault on his identity in ways that many other patients cannot. The treatment becomes part of the cancer experience and it is difficult to extract the symptoms of the disease from the complications of the treatments. It is an uncertain process, with the uncertainty initially born in the lack of knowledge associated with cancer causation. Armed with what knowledge we have about causation, people tend to accept blame for engaging in behaviours which put them at risk of cancer. They are doubly burdened by the historically located stigma associated with cancer which depicts the disease as an evil growth, and the more recent public health messages which suggest we can prevent cancer. These messages are necessary because, to a large extent, we *can* prevent many cancers, but they are a double-edged sword cutting away some cancers while aggravating the blame associated with a cancer diagnosis. Psychological theories of cancer causation which highlight cancer personalities also suggest susceptibility and self-blame (Pollock 1993).

Cancer forces each sufferer to confront the meanings associated with the disease—for each sufferer, cancer may be just bad luck or it may be a warning symbol (Dodds 1997). About half of those diagnosed with cancer will survive the disease, but that also means that half of those diagnosed will eventually die of the cancer. For the period of time after a cancer diagnosis, cancer sufferers and their families and friends will be subject to an emotional whirlpool of hope, uncertainty and fear. Even those who survive will never get over cancer and the disease identity and stigma will hang over the heads of the individual and their family (Muzzin et al. 1994). If any good can be identified in a terminal cancer prognosis, it is that the sufferer may be able to acknowledge the dying process and start to prepare for death. Yet this in itself is not straightforward, and issues of awareness and control over dying are different for each person and subject to a number of social, cultural, clinical and ethical considerations, as I discuss in other chapters. It is important that we comprehend the complications of a cancer death as so many people now die of cancer. The symptoms of the various cancers are complex enough, but the disease itself is a bigger and uglier problem. It may, as Kleinman (1988, p. 21) suggests, be that cancer intensifies our awareness of the dangers of our times and of the role of humankind in promulgating such misery.

four

Constructions of a good death

As humans, we cannot escape the fact that we will die. However, there are many ways of dying and with each way there are multiple meanings of death that are expressed individually and culturally. These understandings are social constructs, for we can never really know what death is like until we have experienced it for ourselves. In thinking about death, many people construct an ideal death—well-known examples include 'dying in one's sleep', 'dying on the job' and 'dying with one's boots on'. These ideals draw upon representations of good and bad ways of dying and they are found in many cultures (Bradbury 1996, p. 84). While these representations may share similar social functions to some extent, their actual foundations and manifestations are quite diverse. Representations of good and bad deaths are closely related to cultural and religious belief and to historical context. In a contemporary context, Smith (1993) suggests that it is only in retrospect that we can have confidence in affirming a particular death as 'good'. We are therefore reliant on our observations and our imaginations to help us construct both good and bad deaths. As most people in contemporary Western society are unlikely to observe many deaths, they are only able, in most cases, to imagine what dying and death are like. In this chapter I discuss some of the constructions of a good death. This background provides a framework for understanding how a group of health professionals who observe dying on a daily basis construct an ideal good death. These professional people, who work in hospices and palliative care organisations, have constructed a purposeful ideology of a good death. However, many also recognise the huge gaps that exist between ideals and realities and reconstruct the notion of a good death in terms of a 'good enough death'. With this revision, they acknowledge that 'people die very much as they have lived' (Kellehear 1994, p. 188).

Palliative care philosophy proposes that dying and mourning are 'normal' parts of life. This attempt to normalise death challenges the silence that has surrounded dying and death in the recent past. The health professionals who work in palliative care believe that their patients can be aware of their dying, prepared for death and peaceful in their final acceptance of death and closure of life. A death of this kind is considered good, and whereas denial, anger and resistance to death are not necessarily 'bad', they are not ideal and may, in certain contexts, be merely 'good enough'. This 'good enough' reconstruction is a means by which those caring for terminally ill people do not simply focus on philosophies and attitudes, but rather acknowledge the disruption caused by dying and death. The good death is seen as an ideal, which is at times realised and at other times disputed. As Des Aulniers (1993, p. 41) has noted, the pre-death experience is 'subject to contradictions and chaos' in which no one experiences the 'smoothness of some pre-established pattern which would lead to the final acceptance of death'. The good death is therefore a theory or a model which must be, in the words of Kastenbaum and Thuell (1995, p. 175), 'contextualised' in order to be 'more inclusive, integrated and helpful to caregivers'.

CAN DEATH BE GOOD?

The notion of a good death may sound oxymoronic to many people living in contemporary Western societies. These societies are infused with cultural assumptions about illness, disease and death; health is beautiful and good, aligned closely to perfection, whereas disease and death are imperfect and implicitly bad (Gilman 1995). However, throughout history, people have attempted to distinguish between 'good' and 'bad' deaths (Prior 1989, p. 48). From an anthropological perspective, a good death is 'one which suggests some mastery over the arbitrariness of the biological occurrence' (Bloch & Parry 1982, p. 15). This means that people desire to make sense of what is happening, to avoid the accidental and premature death, and to construct cultural means to express their sociality in the face of their ultimate finitude. Our individual fragile lives are made stronger in the process of shared meaning about life and death. Berger (1967) follows this reasoning, suggesting that the construction of meaning around death is an essentially social, communal phenomenon.

Nevertheless, this can pose problems for people living in contemporary societies who are 'bereft of a communally acknowledged model of a good death' (Mellor & Schilling 1993, p. 423). How can people in these societies develop 'a viable art of dying appropriate to twentieth-century values and medical realities' (Hunsaker Hawkins 1991, p. 301)?

The term 'good death' can mean many things, particularly in the context of contemporary Western societies. It may have a literal interpretation—for example, when it is related to euthanasia (Veatch 1976, p. 5; Saclier 1976). While this use fell from favour for some time, recent proponents of assisted suicide and other kinds of euthanasia have again proposed the association (Humphrey 1991, p. 30). Aries (1981) has linked a good death with an 'acceptable' way of dying, but of course what is acceptable in one context may not be in another, and in many ways this is not a particularly useful term for present-day sociological analysis. The list of what is acceptable in various contexts may be particularly exhaustive, although Weisman (1978, p. 193) proposes several factors that focus on how the physical, psychological and social well-being of the individual who is dying might be maintained. A person who dies an 'appropriate death' should have his or her suffering reduced and be relieved from pain. Attention should also be given to encouraging that person, within the limits of his or her disability, to function on as high a level as possible. Attempts should be made to help the terminally ill person resolve residual conflicts and his or her wishes should be fulfilled where possible. Choice is of particular importance, and this includes the opportunity to yield control to others and the possibility of seeking or relinquishing significant key people. Weisman's definition of a good death follows the modern concern that the individual should be encouraged to explore various choices. It does not consider whether death should be good for those who must observe the dying person, or those who are called upon to facilitate the viable choices.

Other scholars have pursued a similar way of considering what a good death might mean. Walter (1994, p. 59) suggests that, while 'traditional' good deaths involve farewells to family and preparation for the after-life, and 'modern' good deaths should be quick and painless, the 'postmodern' good death means dying 'my own way'. The postmodern way of dying is representative of the theory that suggests unitary representations of truth are replaced by a plurality of viewpoints. Young and Cullen (1996) follow this kind of theory partially, by proposing that dying people engage in various emotional and behavioural strategies typifying four approaches to death (rational, spiritual, humorous and poetic) to create their own good deaths. It is important to acknowledge the degree to which the cultural preoccupation with individuality has influenced popular discourse about dying and death, as well as professional rhetoric and practice in the management of dying and death. There are many popular narratives of the good death depicted in fiction and non-fiction literature, film and television, in newspapers and theatre. 'Indeed, we seem to have replaced the tendency to ignore death with the tendency to generate a plurality of concepts about it.' (Hunsaker Hawkins 1991) Health professionals who care for dying and bereaved people are encouraged to be open to the different views about what might constitute a good death. These might be influenced by concepts such as age at death, place of death, cultural beliefs, 'anticipatory grief', and beliefs about euthanasia and advanced directives (Katz & Sidell 1994).

Of the recent sociological attempts to analyse and describe the social life of the dying person, Kellehear's work on the good death (1990) is most notable for its comprehensive account of how 100 people organised their lives in the year before they died. He identified awareness of dying, social adjustments and personal preparations, public preparations, arrangements relating to work and farewells as the five key features of the good death for people who are dying from cancer. While this perspective features the individual, it also concentrates on the interactions that person has with their various social contacts. Kellehear's good death model also makes reference to the shared understanding of death and the public ritual that are still, to some extent, present in modern industrialised societies. The preparation of a will and the funeral feature as part of the public preparations that people make for their future deaths. It is, of course, notable that these people were dying from cancer and, as Field (1996) has argued, people who are dying from other chronic diseases with less certain trajectories may not follow similar patterns of developing awareness of approaching death. Both Field and Kellehear draw upon the sociological tradition of Glaser and Strauss (1966, 1968, 1971) to establish the importance of awareness in modern dying trajectories. Further sociological studies have used this central concept to explore the extent to which awareness of dying can be used practically in therapeutic interactions as well as politically within movements concerned with the management of death (Williams 1989; Seale 1991; Costain Schou 1993; Timmermans 1994).

Some accounts construct types of good deaths by combining elements of what Walter (1994) would call traditional, modern and postmodern deaths. Hunsaker Hawkins (1991) suggests 'ritual death', 'victorious death', and 'one's own death' are three potential versions of the 'art of dying for our time'. Scripts for dying are proposed by Seale (1995) as a way of showing how individuals seek to imbue dying with meaning in contemporary society. He counterpoises 'heroic death', as it is proclaimed by experts, with rival scripts that are employed by individuals who avoid open awareness and discussion of death. Yet other deaths, such as those of the very old and confused and unexpected deaths, cannot be scripted. In her study on death and bereavement in the London area, Bradbury

(1993, 1996) discovered a huge variation in descriptions of what made a death good or bad. Although acknowledging this variation, she groups both good and bad deaths into three broad types: the sacred, the medical and the natural. It appears that all three types are closely related and usually present in combination and in an ever-changing presentation (1996, p. 87). This last point is important, as it acknowledges that the pre-death experience is, in reality, subject to contradictions and chaos. Yet sociological and cultural analysis can lead to some important insights about how death is given meaning, and about how the mysterious and the uncertain is made more tangible for those who must confront suffering and loss.

Kearl (1996, p. 340) notes that aging and dying well involve both the individual's own strategies for developing a sense of well-being and the social recognition of their attempts. A central concern in Kearl's discussion of dying well is changing attitudes to death in the modern world. Rather than fearing premature death, many people, particularly those approaching old age, may fear the postmature demise. According to Kearl, deaths become good 'when they serve not only the needs of the dying but also those of their survivors and of the broader social orders as well' (1996, p. 345). He suggests that the perspective of the individual is just one way of considering whether a death can be considered good. The dying person's significant others and the broader society are considered in Kearl's suggested framework, so deaths are good when 'they enhance the social solidarities or in other ways contribute to the well-being of the living' (1996, p. 346). My own work on the good death in palliative care organisations (McNamara et al. 1994, 1995), which I will discuss in this chapter, demonstrates how good deaths can facilitate the functioning of the organisation by reducing the physical and emotional labour of the staff who care for terminally ill people.

THE GOOD DEATH IN HOSPICE AND PALLIATIVE CARE

The good death is an ideology which, in the past, served as the central organising philosophical concern of the hospice movement (Palgi & Ambramovitch 1984; Rinaldi & Kearl 1990; Clark & Seymour 1999). I believe this philosophical concern has been replaced with a new vision that encourages health professionals to accept the limitations of open awareness and shared decision-making, issues which I discuss in Chapter 7 and Chapter 8. This change in focus has also mirrored the change from the original social movement of hospice to the practice of palliative care, which is now proposed within the mainstream of health care. However, in order to understand this change in focus, it is necessary to establish how the good death has been associated with the original

JET LIBRARY

hospice movement. Taylor's (1993a, 1993b) work with Australian palliative care nurses examines the meaning of a good death from the
perspective of the nurses. Death is identified as a continuous social event,
perceived as 'good' if it goes well overall. It is important that support
is given and trust gained, that effective symptom control is achieved and
that the nurse's involvement makes a difference. The palliative care nurses
in her study clearly saw that it was their job to help facilitate a good
death. Other features of a good death have been identified in research
conducted in hospices and palliative care organisations. These include:
control on the part of the person who is dying (Logue 1994); awareness
of the approaching death by both the terminally ill person and their
family; open discussion and acceptance of the death by all concerned;
and some kind of closure which involves settling both practical and
interpersonal 'business' (McNamara et al. 1994).

The good deaths that happen in palliative care settings are often
contrasted with those experienced in different contexts, particularly those
that happen in large hospitals where many palliative care professionals
believe death is medicalised and institutionalised. Although this tendency
to contrast does not indicate that good deaths only happen when patients
receive palliative care, the contrast becomes part of the definition of the
good death. Ramsay (1975, p. 82) argues that the distinction or contrast
indicates that good deaths are relational. He believes that 'good' and
'death' are contradictions in terms, but suggests that the predicate 'good'
is still applicable 'in contrast to worse ways to die and worse ways to
grieve or not to grieve'. In Chapter 9, I discuss the experiences of some
palliative care nurses that originally led them to this kind of nursing.
Many of these experiences indicate disillusionment with mainstream
medicine and, on some occasions, produce an outspoken criticism of
curative-based medicine employed in terminal illness. This kind of
motive is evident not only in nurses, but also in doctors and allied health
professionals. I interviewed Michael, a general practitioner, who spoke
about his early training in large teaching hospitals where he told me the
consultants were 'a shower of bastards' who were 'bad at teaching
students and bad at talking to patients'. Most of the time, Michael felt
disillusioned at having to be part of the inappropriate treatments measured
out to patients, which only seemed to cause more suffering. However,
he did not lose all hope, saying: 'At the end of the day you ask
yourself—can you do something to make a difference?'

In the context of palliative care, the good death is obviously an
idealised concept. Within this distinctive culture of caregiving, death is
not considered bad, but a natural part of life to be accepted when it
comes, even if the death may at times be premature. The good death,
therefore, is a process where the terminally ill person, their family and
the health professional team share a mutual acceptance of the terminally

ill person's approaching death and engage in shared decision-making. It does not relate to the single moment of death, but to a complex set of relations and preparations whereby some degree of closure and peace can be achieved for all concerned. Nimocks and colleagues (1987, p. 329) suggest a definition which accommodates all of the social actors in the process. They suggest that 'goodness' involves the way that all of the 'interactants accept the impending death, receive emotional care and support, mitigate the dying person's discomfort and isolation and complete all the unfinished business'. Field (1989) considers that 'good' communication and joint decision-making regarding the patient's care are necessary elements of a 'good' death experience. These kinds of observations fit very well into the current interest in patient empowerment. Kelner and Bourgeault (1993) indicate that health professionals must concede their autonomy, accommodate the patient's wishes to have more control over dying and enter into a partnership with patients in the decision-making process.

The manner in which the good death is understood in the palliative care context, as outlined above, follows Kearl's model of a good death (1996)—not only is the dying person considered, but also the social circle around that person, as well as the society in which that person lives. This definition suggests norms and rules for living and dying which aim to make people comfortable with the idea of death, but the norms and rules surrounding a good death also impose a form of social control. While choices can be made, it is implicit that these choices should facilitate awareness, openness and acceptance. These latter three concepts are the core of the good death model of the hospice movement and draw heavily upon the sociological ideas of Glaser and Strauss (1966, 1968, 1971) and the stages of dying theory of Kubler-Ross (1969, 1975). Ideologically, the good death serves two purposes. First, the occurrence affirms the socially responsible patient who quietly slips away once the health professionals have fulfilled their roles in preparing that person for death. Second, it benefits palliative care administrative structures by supporting their philosophies and goals and by facilitating the smooth running of the organisations. Deaths that are 'bad' not only traumatise the lives of the terminally ill people and their families, they also challenge the goals of the palliative care model and complicate organisational maintenance. Bad deaths also drain resources, as greater time is spent in care and discussion amongst the staff who are often physically and emotionally exhausted by the experience. The good death establishes a degree of stability within the growing institutions of hospice and palliative care by providing precedents relating to normative behaviours. However, the ideal also potentially implies rigidity of definitions and limitations to spontaneity and, in effect, presents challenges to those men and women who care for terminally ill people and their families through their work in palliative care services.

DEATH: GOOD OR 'GOOD ENOUGH'?

The good death has served as a core symbol within the philosophy of hospice and palliative care over the past 30 years, but it is important to acknowledge that this symbol is open to debate and that it changes over time. The shifting definitions of what is considered a good death must be seen from the perspective of the patient, the family and the health professionals who work with terminally ill people. I have already established that good deaths can mean a number of different things to different people and it is interesting that, even within the context of palliative care, what is considered good is not always clear. Payne and colleagues (1996) have shown that health professionals' perceptions of what makes a good death are very different from those of the patients in the palliative care unit where their study was conducted. In my own research I have found variation in perceptions within the group of palliative care nurses and other health professionals. Many of these health professionals speak of the need for excellent standards of care and adequate symptom control. They aim to provide holistic care and comfort to both patients and their families, and work towards providing an environment where the patient may die peacefully and with dignity. Many of these concerns feature in their 'good death stories', which are often shared in formal and informal meetings in palliative care settings. It seems important, from the health professional's perspective, to be involved in the patient's dying trajectory, as one very experienced nurse, Jacqui, commented: 'It's a good death when you feel comfortable with the scenario . . . when you feel you've participated.'

When asked to define a good death, many health professionals do, however, display a degree of hesitancy, as the comment of another nurse, Alexis, illustrates:

> It's a nebulous term; when we talk about it we know what we mean—we like to have the symptoms controlled and hopefully to have the patient come to terms with their death, but inevitably most patients will ask at some time 'why me?'

Another senior nurse and administrator, Angela, paused before attempting a definition and said:

> Oh dear . . . I suppose it's when everything goes well—but it's not a perfect world in here and often things don't go well . . . you know the

patients bring the real world here with them and we don't work in a vacuum.

Some health professionals felt uncomfortable with 'labelling' the different kinds of dying experiences and acknowledged the importance of not imposing their own values upon patients and their families. Linda cautioned that they needed to 'step back' and 'respect the different ways of dying'. The elements of patient autonomy and accommodation to individual and family value systems feature as aspects of the good death experience. From the health professional's perspective, the good death is an ideal situation for all concerned in the dying process. When all 'goes well', the patients, families and health professionals have participated in a good death experience. Although the health professionals are aware of the factors that inhibit good deaths, their stories indicate a level of idealisation, the story often working to shape the event rather than the events shaping the stories. The good death, although not always readily achieved, is something they work towards implicitly.

Many further features work to shift the conceptualisation of the good death in the context of palliative care. Concerns have been expressed in both Britain and the United States that some hospices have not been able to maintain their initial high ideals and standards of care (Abel 1986; Seale 1989). James and Field (1992) document changes within Britain, focusing on the increasing bureaucratisation and professionalisation of the hospice movement. More recently, Bradshaw (1996) has argued that an emotivist culture has replaced the original spiritual dimension of hospice, thus shifting the focus towards an efficiency-based medicalised model. Corner and Dunlop (1997, p. 288) identify three defining features which cast doubt over the direction of British palliative care: a loss of radicalism characteristic of early hospice care; the exclusive nature of palliative care, which has narrowed the range of diseases and needs treated; and the impact of medicalisation within palliative care. Siebold (1992) considers the future of the hospice movement in the United States, highlighting the paradoxical aims of this form of supportive care—to humanise dying and to pursue further technology to ease the pain of death. Furthermore, the degree to which terminally ill people are empowered—or even able to engage in shared decision-making—in the last weeks and months of their lives has been open to question (Logue 1994; Mesler 1995). It is notable that different concerns seem to emanate from different parts of the world. The British critique concentrates on the organisation and delivery of care and the professionalisation and medicalisation of hospice care (Clark & Seymour 1999), whereas the focus in the United States appears to be upon issues of increasing technology and the degree to which people are able to control their own dying. These trends do not merely reflect the research culture of the respective areas, but also mirror the social and cultural concerns of those nations. Australian palliative care is in turn influenced by both Britain and the United States, though the greater influence appears to come from Britain.

Critique of the good death in palliative care has come not just from the safer distances of academia, but also from within, from the actions of terminally ill people who resist the 'hospice ritual', and from the professionals who express dissatisfaction with this philosophical emphasis. An alternative way of looking at the interaction that takes place in the time before death is to propose the idea of a death that is 'good enough'. A 'good enough' death has been described by two prominent palliative care practitioners as a death 'as close as possible to the circumstances the person would have chosen' (Campbell 1990, p. 2) and 'a death with integrity, consistent with the life that person has led' (Ashby in Komesaroff et al. 1995, p. 597). These kinds of definitions reflect the realities of patients' lives, as not all terminally ill people use the time before death to resolve past issues and say their farewells. In fact, this time may be spent, in the words of Max, a palliative care doctor, 'going in and out of the idea of dying'. My own experiences with patients confirm what many palliative care health professionals have told me. A patient may be depressed and ready to die and yet on another day, or even later in the same day, they may be found complaining about how the expected visitors are late. Ted, the very first patient I helped look after, responded to my initial greeting, 'How are you feeling today?' with the comment, 'If I had a gun I would shoot myself.' Over the next week, Ted proceeded to take an inordinate interest in his meals so that he could 'build himself up'. Marjorie, a palliative care doctor, told me she thought 'at least half, or even more, of our patients are ambivalent and we have to be available to allow them to change their minds'. I have had several nurses tell me that they would encourage the patient to express his or her rage, even until death. The kind of rebellion, depicted in the Dylan Thomas poem 'Do not go gentle into that good night', fits quite well with the individualistic ethos of the 'good enough death', and yet it seems far removed from the peaceful and dignified 'good death'.

In many ways, the conflicting understandings of what is 'good' or otherwise are what have prompted professionals who work in palliative care to articulate new definitions which accommodate the variation in perspectives. These include allowing patients to have the choice in deciding where they think is the most appropriate place to die. Jo, a palliative care nurse, said: 'Put it this way, we might think the hospice is *the* place to die, neat and tidy and all, but it may not be where the patient wants to be.' Another nurse, Emily, who I accompanied on visits to patients in their own homes, spoke about one patient who we had seen that evening and who had subsequently gone by ambulance to hospital:

> You know Mrs Thompson will probably die tonight in hospital, poor love. If she hadn't gone she may have bled to death at home. Who's to say she didn't have a good death . . . the family were the kind of people that expected everything to be done, you know sirens blaring, tubes and monitors, that's 'good' to them.

In this example, Emily is shifting the definition of what is 'good' to what the patient and the family wants. The death would not have been considered good if we apply the norms implicit in the traditional hospice good death. However, by focusing on the individual—and, in this example, the close family circle—rather than on the broad social collective, the death is reconstructed as 'good enough'.

These kinds of interpretations are consistent with the theoretical position that authority over dying should be invested in the individual. The central focus upon the dying individual can be linked to the processes of individualisation and privatisation in contemporary society. Mellor (1993, pp. 21–22) comments on the individualisation present within British hospices:

> Death may be present in [the] hospice in a way that it is not in the hospital, but its presence remains a predominantly personally located one. It is notable that the strategies for dying associated with the hospice movement . . . are directed towards *individuals*, encouraging them to construct some sort of individual awareness of the meaningfulness of their lives and deaths. They therefore offer nothing to counteract the widespread privatisation of meaning in high modernity which is the major source of many persons' contemporary difficulties in dealing with death.

A 'good enough' death ideology may be thought of as a realistic and humanistic perspective that is person-centred and empowering. Yet closer examination of the concept reveals that acceptance of the 'good enough' ethic can also shift the locus of responsibility. The concept of a 'good enough' death embraces uncertainty, potentially releasing people from the rules by which they live and die. However, while in principle the idea that everyone can construct their own scripts for dying holds appeal for members of a highly individualistic society, the rhetoric of a 'good enough' death can mask less positive aspects of these scripts. Closer examination of the concept reveals that acceptance of the 'good enough' ethic can shift the locus of responsibility from the social collective (and the professional carers) to the individual who is dying. If the death of the person who is terminally ill does not go well, the 'good enough' ethic allows health professionals to rationalise the failures in terms of the dying person's decisions rather than in terms of failures on the part of the organisation that manages the person's death. Thinking about the dying process in this manner can minimise the necessity of reflection about the quality and the meaning of care.

CONCLUSION

It appears that criticisms can be levelled at both the good death ethic and the more pragmatic philosophy that proposes a 'good enough' death. Where the good death could be construed as too prescriptive, the 'good enough' death may be so loosely constructed that it lacks shared meaning. Both constructions of death highlight our fragile lives in different ways, but are we, as humans in contemporary society, in a 'no-win' situation, caught betwixt and between traditional ritual and mores and a kind of postmodern anarchy of belief? Contemporary social responses to dying and death reflect the kinds of uncertainties that may exist for individuals. The 'experts', who include doctors, ethicists, politicians and clergy, cannot provide answers, failing to reach agreement on technical and moral questions of length and quality of life—and indeed on what constitutes a good death. Medicine has mostly responded to the problem of death by postponing it, as discussed in Chapter 6. However, sometimes medicine is incorporated into a more holistic approach to the care of terminally ill people, as we have seen in the hospice movement and the continuing practice of palliative care. Originally the contemporary hospice movement sought to reintroduce a ritual for dying. The good death, proposed a manner of dying in which open communication and acceptance of death were actively encouraged. Dying a good death, however, does not always happen and the good death is an ideal that has become increasingly inappropriate in the current social climate of 'patient empowerment' and 'consumer choice'.

Individual choice has become a principal organising symbol in contemporary Western society, and it follows that this ethic has influenced ideology within the palliative care movement. The philosophy of a 'good enough' death is a compromise that allows for the ethical principle of patient autonomy, but also acknowledges the realities of patients' experiences. However, this complex notion does not simply mean that patients are 'empowered' by health professionals to take control of their dying. It is therefore imperative that the actual context of patient experience is examined in relation to the organisational maintenance of the institutions that manage terminally ill people. A good death in contemporary society is not just a matter of 'dying my own way', as Walter (1994) suggests. Terminally ill people rely on the care of health professionals and on the services provided within the health care system.

It is therefore necessary to be conscious both of the personal circumstances of the individual and of the form of justice that is proclaimed and enacted within the institutions that are entrusted with the fragile lives of dying people.

five

How we die: The uncertain worlds of terminally ill people

Dying is an uncertain and frightening process for terminally ill people and their families and close friends. The uncertainty surrounding dying and death makes us all fragile, but none more so than the terminally ill people themselves. Much of the literature about dying and death avoids the painful and personal approach of discussing the actual experience of dying, although there are a few notable exceptions (Kellehear 1990; Nuland 1993). It seems far easier to research and write about attitudes to death, or the way that health professionals care for dying people. While we can learn a great deal about death from these indirect approaches to the subject, they do not really address the question of how people die. This chapter focuses on the personal and social worlds of terminally ill people, for it is through attempting to understand these worlds that we begin to understand how people die. Obviously people die in many different ways and for various reasons. I do not attempt to deal with these variations here, but rather discuss some of the sociological patterns and theories that contribute to an integrative framework for understanding the dying person. Integrative frameworks combine various disciplinary perspectives in order to explain phenomena in an holistic way. To understand the personal and social worlds of dying people, we must consider the interconnections of body, spirit and selfhood within a broader sociocultural context.

Terminally ill people are not discrete entities separate from their social networks, but people whose psychic and relational boundaries are negotiated with those around them. These negotiations may also extend to incorporeal dimensions and to nature if these are significant to the individual's world-view. Some people may live quite isolated lives, while others are closely involved in relationships of interdependence. Most importantly, the individual person or 'self' is not an entity, separate and independent from his or her biological body. The body is both social and biological, 'natural' and 'cultural' (Turner 1984, 1992; Fox 1993). A significantly changed body contributes to a significantly changed self. The terminally ill person's sense of identity and their ability to cope with illness experiences (particularly in the case of terminal illness) also continue to be linked to past experiences or 'life themes' (Zlatin 1995) and to their social location within society. The dying person's agency, therefore, will be filtered to various degrees, by their place within the broader socio-demographic fabric of society. Gender, ethnicity, age, educational achievements and occupational status will all have some bearing on the capacity each person has to control their own circumstances. Serious illness of any kind is disruptive and disabling; however, terminal illness magnifies this disruption and disablement to such an extent that the failure of the body becomes the focus of attention. In this chapter, I take the failure of the body as a starting point to discuss the various components of the terminally ill person's personal and social world.

THE FAILURE OF THE BODY

Social scientists who write about health and illness have been criticised for ignoring the basic physicality of humans. These kinds of criticisms have sparked a recent interest in 'the body' and in theories of embodiment. Kelly and Field (1996, pp. 250–51) suggest that bringing the body into analytical focus helps us to see the interplay between self and identity and to 'manage sociologically the relation between biological and social facts'. Embodiment theory supports this perspective by proposing 'that the body as a methodological figure must itself be non-dualistic, i.e., not distinct from or in interaction with an opposed principle of mind' (Csordas 1990, p. 8). Dying 'bodies' are particularly problematic because they are decaying and obstreperous and betray the healthy self. The dying body is out of control, refusing to be shaped to the ideal. In general, the body is used in many ways to aestheticise the 'interior' self and through the body we express our common bonds with other people. The body, therefore, is instrumental in developing self-identity. When the body begins to break down irretrievably, identity is spoiled (Goffman

1963) and the dying person begins to take on a new life and new identity associated with terminal illness. Bodily discipline is intrinsic to the competent social agent (Giddens 1991), so it seems that dying people who cannot control their bodily functions risk the label of incompetence. Their bodies hold the power to explain their situation, with deterioration holding clues to the gradual loss of self and life.

Each terminally ill person engages with a unique set of factors that alter his or her own conceptions of self. One of the most immediate and urgent factors, often dominating the experience of illness and approaching death, is the set of symptoms associated with the illness. Palliative care professionals cite weakness and fatigue as the most disabling symptoms of terminal illness and unfortunately there is little that can be done to alleviate them. This manifestation of terminal illness is just one of the many symptoms which influence the dying person's conception of themselves. Nausea, vomiting, breathlessness, constipation, diarrhoea, oedema (swelling), smell from infections and wounds, confusion and pain are also associated variously with disease (especially cancer) and with intervention procedures. The body, in these instances, is truly out of control and it threatens the sufferer's sense of self. People who talk about their symptoms also mention their 'loss of dignity', a factor which is closely linked to their inability to monitor and control their bodily functions. Their tumours, for example, may erupt on the surface of the body. Their skin tone and colour changes, they become wasted and the insides of their bodies, particularly their bones, become more visible from the outside. These bodily disfigurements are all the more dangerous and powerful because they are symbols of finitude.

The story of Frank, a 72-year-old man with cancer, illustrates how many terminally ill people change through the circumstances of their disease. Rather than intellectualising their existential crisis, they engage in a bodily expression of control and lack of control. The bodily deterioration both changes their capacity to act and, as in the following case, prompts further action to attempt to contain the bodily expression of deterioration. Frank was worried that he had become too sleepy from his medication to be able to control his colostomy (an opening in the colon, surgically fixed on to the abdominal wall, which empties into an attached bag). The smell associated with the accidents, which had begun to happen since his colon cancer had progressed, distressed him. Frank's distress was deepened by the knowledge that his fastidious wife did not want to care for him. The colostomy bag exploded one evening, much to Frank's horror, and he made the decision to do what he could to control the situation. Some of the hospice staff who cared for Frank were surprised to learn that he had arranged for a man who they called 'Hernia Bob' to come into the hospice to measure him for an expensive truss. For some unexplained reason, Frank thought the truss would help control the smell, and prevent the spillage from the colostomy bag. The staff were sceptical about the benefits of such a device, particularly as Frank was beginning to approach the terminal phase of his illness. However, they did try to hide their opinions from Frank who, in his desperation, was prepared to try anything.

Frank's story reflects the despair experienced by many cancer sufferers. Their bodies are inscribed not just with disease, but also with the 'cultural values' that are associated with disease (Csordas 1994). In Frank's case, his ability to make decisions was significantly altered by the progression of his disease. He was fighting to maintain control; his deteriorating body was a sign that he, as a person, was deteriorating. He was also strongly motivated to hide the signs of his deterioration as he was embarrassed and feared his lack of social acceptability. DiGiacomo (1987, p. 319), an anthropologist who has written about her own experience with Hodgkin's disease (a cancer of the lymphatic system) describes how, in the hospital, her identity was 'assailed', not just through the process of total institutionalisation, but through the heavy 'symbolic charge' associated everywhere with cancer. Murphy (1987, p. 90), another anthropologist writing of his experience of a tumour in his spine, which eventually led to quadriplegia, suggests that serious disability takes over all other 'claims to social standing' and becomes not just a 'role', but an 'identity'.

Bodily deterioration is also a sign of approaching death. Knowledge of approaching death—whether this is implicit or explicit—and its associated grief, further complicates self-knowledge and the capacity to act to change circumstances. Often terminally ill people express concerns that they are a burden and that they cannot do anything for themselves. Many patients are truly embarrassed by their distressing symptoms, which mean that professional carers must attend to distasteful jobs such as cleaning up vomit, urine and faeces. Stanley, a fellow hospice patient of Frank, had tears in his eyes as he explained how the nurses had to feed him, shower him and even take him to the toilet. He said he would prefer to die than face the embarrassment of 'having his bum wiped' by someone young enough to be his granddaughter. The patients' inability to care for themselves signals the relinquishing of control and the beginning of a social death, whereby they cease to be significant social actors able to participate in the world of the living (Sudnow 1967; Kastenbaum 1977; Mulkay 1993; Sweeting & Gilhooly 1997). In this context, the social death happens at some time before the biological death, when the terminally ill person ceases to interact with others in a socially meaningful way. Of course, not all patients withdraw like this; many act in a self-sufficient manner until they die. Nevertheless, the important point here is that disabling symptoms lead to lack of control and no one can ever be sure of the symptoms they will have—they are burdens distributed unequally and with no regard for the virtues of the undeserving.

No person remains unchanged by the experience of severe illness and approaching death. Some people stubbornly persist in trying to do things for themselves, while others willingly relinquish control. In the case of terminal illness, many people also become confused and suffer significant cognitive impairment. When terminally ill people become unable to make decisions for themselves, it falls upon their families and their professional carers to decide how the person will be treated. I witnessed a nurse, Jo, caring for Aldo, a patient who, through the progression of his disease, had lost the capacity to communicate in any meaningful way. He became severely distressed if he did not have a small square cloth crunched in his hand which he held up to his face. On other occasions he insisted on writing down all the details of conversations and surroundings: the names of the persons present, what they were wearing, the medications he was given and any other minutia that he considered important. Jo explained that Aldo had most probably suffered a previous compulsive disorder, which had been exacerbated by the stress associated with his terminal illness. Any insight Aldo may have had into his approaching death was fractured by his need to record the small details of his passing life. Here Aldo's memories and past experiences incapacitated him, yet in other situations patients are enriched by reflections upon their past lives in ways that allow them to experience a good death.

SPIRITUAL DIMENSIONS

The spiritual needs of terminally ill people seem to be the least understood. This is hardly surprising in an increasingly secular society (Walter 1994) where both dying and death are regulated by the state and subsumed within scientific discourses (Prior 1989). As Doyle, a world-renowned authority on palliative care, states: 'It is surely clear that I believe we should be concerned about spiritual matters as they affect our patients. Whether or not we have looked at them is a different thing.' (1992, p. 310) Conventional aspects of religion and spirituality are also more readily understood and accepted than the unusual or challenging elements of these dimensions. In Australia, the Indigenous population is the most striking example of dying patients whose spiritual needs are misunderstood. There is often a cultural gap of understanding between the recipients and the providers of care. Research conducted in the northwest of Australia (Williamson 1996) indicates that the most important issue for Aboriginal people is the need to die in their own 'country'. Most Aboriginal people accept that family members who are very ill may have to be taken from their country for treatment, but there was a strong opinion expressed in this study that, where possible, they should return to their country for the last few months or weeks of their lives. Many terminally ill Aboriginal people simply do not present to medical services and many others abscond from hospital to return to their homes. Their spiritual connectedness to their land and family is of prime importance, overriding the need for medical care.

Nina's story is also somewhat atypical, but as is often the case in sociological analysis—and indeed in life—the anomaly teaches us something more about common humanity. Nina was a Buddhist nun who was terminally ill after the course of a long illness and treatment regime, which included extensive surgery to drain fluid from her chest cavity and remove parts of a tumour from her lungs. In accordance with her religious beliefs, she did not wish to take medications that would influence her state of mind and prevent her from confronting her suffering. Nina had used conventional kinds of treatment and support but had now organised her own support system to help her prepare for death. Nina died in the inpatient hospice where I conducted some of my fieldwork, but unfortunately I did not have the opportunity to see her before she died. However, I spoke to Andrew, a nurse who was involved in her care. Andrew prided himself on a broad knowledge of other cultural and spiritual beliefs and told me that he had long talks with Nina before she died. Andrew spoke about Nina's attempts to prepare for death in the Buddhist way by experiencing the various signs of dying while she was still alive. Andrew said that it was important for Nina to have a sense of awareness, but this was partially influenced by her eventual decision to use morphine to help control a particularly difficult pain.

Nina was not conscious when she died, but gradually deteriorated over the course of several hours. She did not achieve her aim of staying conscious until death, but her brave attempt gave meaning to her last days. Nina's experience illustrates how body and 'spirit' or mind are inter-connected. We may be tempted to interpret Nina's struggle as a failure of the 'mind' to control the 'body'. However, as Csordas (1990, p. 8) argues, we need not conceptualise the body in opposition to an abstract principle of the 'mind'. In this sense, pain is not necessarily an evil force we must overcome but something that must be understood and managed appropriately. Illich (1976, p. 271) notes that, in traditional cultures, 'pain was recognised as an inevitable part of the subjective reality of one's own body'. Pain was made tolerable by integrating it into a meaningful setting. Nina actively made her experience meaningful by preparing for death in a way that drew upon both her traditional Buddhist beliefs and the modern technology available to her. This interpretation takes into account the context of time, place and individual circumstance, which includes the pathology and history of the disease.

In the examples of Aboriginal people's spirituality and Nina's commitment to Buddhism, we see the power of religious belief to imbue both life and death with meaning and purpose. Berger (1967, p. 44) associates 'a good death' with religion, because with religious belief the individual is able 'to die while retaining to the end a meaningful relationship with the *nomos* [laws] of one's society—subjectively meaningful to oneself and objectively meaningful in the minds of others'. However, from a secular perspective, 'life has no meaning or purpose other than the goals we set ourselves as individuals or members of a community' (Badham 1996, p. 168). In life, the secular person must find forms of sacredness other than those associated with theistic and nontheistic religious belief. Many people do just this by constructing their own kinds of spirituality and life goals. Discussions with terminally ill people, their families and their professional carers provide a very broad understanding of individual constructions of spirituality. Explanations of spirituality span a vast continuum of understanding, covering relationships with nature and other people and encompassing very different worldviews and notions of self. These explanations often focus on abstract notions such as peace, balance and harmony. I have been told that spirituality is about 'the sanctity of life'; that it involves 'whole relationships with the world and with other people'; that it 'revolves around the person's inner soul'; and that it is about 'life direction and the ability to maintain control of individual beliefs'.

Spirituality, in the context of contemporary 'secular' society, appears to be eclectic, individualistic and not necessarily associated with a 'supernatural world'. However, individual interpretations of organised religion are also not as static as one would expect. In my interviews with terminally ill people, I have found that those who have a strong religious commitment also have more clearly defined beliefs about the meaning of life and death than those people who do not have a strong faith. However, most of the people I have spoken to do not have a strong religious commitment, a finding that reflects the broader population (de Vaus 1996). Some who told me they were Catholic did not believe in heaven or hell, but suggested a more nebulous after-life, and others who said they were of Buddhist background did not have time to go to the temple. Belief in particular religions cannot always be associated with certain ethnic or cultural backgrounds either. A Chinese Malaysian woman had converted from Buddhism to become a Jehovah's Witness and Moi, another Chinese Malaysian woman, had recently converted from Buddhism to become a Baptist. Although Moi said she was of Baptist faith she did not express a great deal of confidence in either Buddhism or Christianity. She said that she preferred to rely upon her own resources and was unsure of any after-life. I believe her comments reflect the way that many people, regardless of ethnic background and nominated religion, approach the terminal phase of their illnesses. Sacred and secular are not binary opposites and many people do not identify with one or the other but are influenced by both. This sacred–secular continuum tends to create a great deal of existential uncertainty, which intensifies our human frailty.

THE TERMINALLY ILL PERSON'S PLACE IN SOCIETY

If we are to understand how people die, it is necessary to understand the degree to which they are able to exercise some control over their circumstances. Each terminally ill person negotiates his or her own illness and dying trajectory with varying degrees of ability and support due to his or her own place in society. The degree to which a terminally ill person has control, or is able to actively engage in decision-making has been linked to age (Rinaldi & Kearl 1990), patient residence and the degree to which staff set limits upon their own involvement with patients and families (Mesler 1995). We must also be aware of the terminally ill person's social location within the broader society. Ethnicity, educational background, occupational status, gender and the kinds of social supports terminally ill people receive all contribute to their social location and must be understood in the light of entrenched social inequalities. Personal issues of suffering and loss need to be cast within a broader spectrum of culture and society and through this we see that death is not the great leveller (Small 1997, p. 202), but rather that we die much as we have lived. Those who have lived a life of disadvantage tend to die in disadvantaged circumstances (Kellehear 1994). They may have access to good medical care, but we must also ask to what extent people are able to understand and utilise the services that are available. Furthermore, how are these people constrained by the social and cultural circumstances of their own lives?

Terminally ill people who come from non-English speaking backgrounds are particularly disadvantaged. During the course of my fieldwork, I was part of a research team which conducted a survey of palliative care practitioners' perceptions of culturally appropriate care (McNamara et al. 1997). We found that palliative care practitioners felt significantly less able to deliver care to people from cultural backgrounds different from their own. This was particularly the case with counselling and spiritual kinds of support, though even elements of symptom management were seen to be more difficult. In these kinds of situations, palliative care practitioners may be less likely to invite the patient and the family to be involved in decisions that are made about their treatment or less likely to adequately determine what the patient and family want. This is illustrated in the case of Mr Grabinski, a Polish patient, who had been in a satisfactory condition until the week prior to his death and was cared for in his home by his wife who did not speak English. Margaret, a palliative care nurse who was part of a team caring for Mr Grabinski, had to determine whether he should go to hospital. Despite her attempts, she was unable to organise an interpreter and a meeting with the family general practitioner before Mr Grabinski eventually went to the hospital in an ambulance. He spent most of the night in the emergency department and died there not long before dawn. Apparently the facsimile with instructions about his condition did not reach the correct department and Margaret angrily suggested that 'faxes get lost there for days'. In a meeting where the palliative care team reviewed the case, no one was entirely sure who should have taken responsibility—the specialist oncologist, the general practitioner or the hospice service. A telephone interpreter service used on a previous occasion with the family was considered inadequate. The palliative care team agreed that they should organise an interpreter to accompany them while they discussed the death with Mr Grabinski's family. 'After all,' Joe, one of the doctors said, 'we may find that the death was acceptable to the family.' 'No,' another doctor, Richard, stated clearly, 'this was inadequate terminal palliative care, there is no question about it.'

Other aspects which contribute to the terminally ill person's ability to decide on aspects of care often relate to a number of socio-demographic variables, such as occupation, educational attainment, income and area of residence, which combine to give some measure of social class. Palliative care in Australia, for example, is available to many (though not all) people within the general population, yet the dynamics of social class also operate on far more subtle levels. Patients with higher educational levels are more able to participate in extended discussions about their care than those with limited educational levels. While many palliative care practitioners are very conscious of trying to provide similar levels of care to all patients regardless of their social standing, I found it interesting, in my observational research, to observe the varying degrees of rapport that were built between practitioner and patient. I watched as Patrick, a very experienced and dedicated doctor, through no deliberate intention, sat for extended periods of time talking with Louis, a retired judge, while he was unable to develop even the most basic level of discussion with a younger patient, Mick, who had a shaven head and several earrings. In this particular instance, the shared social status of the doctor and retired judge helped them to pursue similar communication patterns, and to find some level of agreement on issues regarding autonomy and decision-making. The gap between Patrick and Mick was far greater—the young man did not want to talk to the doctor. When Patrick asked Mick casually, 'How are you feeling mate?'

Mick mumbled, 'Have you ever died before?' and buried his head in his pillow. Mick's mate, who sat by his bed, shared the silence, bearing witness to their common bond by his appearance, his shaven head and his earrings. In these two cases, the age of the patients was not particularly significant: the judge was very old, the doctor middle-aged and the young man in his late twenties. Yet in other instances the age of the patient may have a strong bearing on the dynamics which frame decision-making about life and death.

Generally, if a patient is young, by comparison with most terminally ill people, more effort is made to allow them to have a greater degree of agency in decisions that are made about them. For example, palliative care practitioners accept that young cancer sufferers will usually want to continue their curative therapy for a longer period of time and that young patients may not wish to discuss their future death. As Ballard (1996, p. 9) notes, 'death before the due time is all the more difficult to deal with'. Deaths of older people are expected and considered to be within the 'normal' course of the life span and many older people accept their approaching death. However, not all older patients just lie down and die quietly and many can be angry until the moment of their death. I visited a patient, Mrs Triplet, in her home with Jacqui, a palliative care nurse. Even though Mrs Triplet was 79 and had advanced cancer, she simply refused 'to let go'. Jacqui had tried counselling her on many occasions, but the old lady stubbornly refused to accept that she was about to die. On the occasion we visited, she lay in a semi-comatose state and remained that way until her death two weeks later.

The gender of terminally ill people also affects their interactions with family and professional caregivers. Despite this, the gendered nature of grief (Thompson 1997) and the emotional division of labour associated with dying and grief (Hockey 1997) are rarely discussed. Women, particularly, are reluctant to ask for help and express guilt for putting nurses and other professional and non-professional caregivers 'to trouble'. Yet they are also more willing to engage in extended conversations about their family circumstances than men, who often are reluctant to discuss highly personal issues. However, it would be unwise to overstate these gender stereotypes because the experience of terminal illness can turn stereotypes around. Roles are often reversed as the husband is required to care for his wife, or the son his mother, and the so-called feminine nurturing and sympathetic qualities can be brought poignantly alive in the male relative who must watch his loved one die. Ray was a large man who had been a farmer all his life, but had left the farm to care for his 43-year-old wife, Ellen, in their city flat so she could have ready access to specialised oncology and palliative care services. Ray and I spoke casually as Ruth, the palliative care nurse, gave Ellen an injection before her shower to settle her distressing nausea. When I enquired about

Ray's farm, he looked out the window and said: 'I'm not worried about the farm, it will still be around next year, won't it?' Ray and Ellen, like many couples I met, particularly when I visited them in their homes, appeared not as two individuals, but as an enmeshed pair brought closer together through crisis. They made the decisions together, not through shifts in the balance of power but through love and self-sacrifice for each other.

THE SOCIAL NETWORK AND FAMILY DYNAMICS

> . . . the sequestration of death from public space makes its presence in the personal sphere potentially commanding and threatening. Individuals are likely to experience the tension between the public absence and the private presence particularly strongly when they find themselves alone with the task of not merely constructing meaning, but of even knowing how to act, when they are faced with the deaths of those they care about (Mellor 1993, p. 20).

It is difficult to know how any one family will behave throughout the course of their loved one's terminal illness and after that person's death. Death is now a private concern and there are many uncertainties associated with dying in contemporary society. The secular nature of contemporary Western society contributes to a lack of religious certainty, which may complicate existential distress. In modern times, people have also become doubtful about the all-encompassing power of science, which in turn creates anxiety about the ability of medicine to provide definitive answers to the problems of mortality and suffering (Lupton 1994). There is also a lack of moral certainty, leaving us bereft of definitive guidelines to questions relating to rights to life and death. Families who experience the dying and death of a loved one respond in ways which reflect these uncertainties. Their responses also complicate the process of decision-making regarding the place and time of death, the treatments accorded to the terminally ill person, and the kinds of communications which take place. As terminally ill people become weaker and less able to engage socially, they become more reliant upon the people in their close social network.

Most of the discussions that occur in the palliative care context contain some reference to 'family dynamics'. The usual practice is to try to include the family in the patient's care and to offer support in this practice. Palliative care practitioners seem to start with the general rule that all people prefer to die at home with the family caring for them. However, many families are unable to care for their dying relative at home and this may be for any number of reasons, ranging from the degree of nursing care needed for the terminally ill person to economic constraints which mean family members must continue to work. Some families simply cannot cope with the physical and emotional stress of caring for a dying relative. Others believe that their relative is best cared for in the hospice or the hospital. Not all families are happy, tight-knit units and the stress of caring for relatives with terminal illnesses can cause some families to 'shatter' or even become hostile. Deirdre, a palliative care nurse, reported how she attended a dying person who was very near death, while the two middle-aged sons 'were on the front lawn engaged in an open brawl'. Margaret, another nurse, told the palliative care team meeting how, during the phase when a patient died, the son fainted and the two daughters hyperventilated.

Families often have mixed responses to the timing of their terminally ill relative's death. Some family members openly express a wish for it all to be over, though others can be changeable. Mark, a palliative care doctor, told the story of how one family he had counselled to expect their father's death panicked and, at the last minute, telephoned the oncologist asking to have their father admitted to hospital. Mark said: 'Within hours the man had a drip in and a nasogastric tube coming out of him . . . they said they wouldn't do this, but they have.' Yet Mark also reported how one of the daughters, who is a vet, approached him: 'She said: "If he were a dog he would have been put to death . . ." She was very matter of fact, very blunt, said: "We don't let animals suffer like this".' Some families simply refuse to let their dying relative go. Isabel died at 103 years of age, cared for by her son and daughter who had spent the past 20 years of their lives intent on keeping Isabel alive. Phillip, a palliative care doctor, said in all seriousness: 'The family wanted to break records, they wanted her to get to 105 or 108 . . . it's been the focus of their lives looking after mum . . . they tried to resuscitate her with cardiac massage . . . even wanted the nurse to resuscitate her further.'

It is often not the terminally ill person who makes the decisions about what happens to them, but the family and the health professionals who care for them. Felicity, a social worker, organised a family meeting to discuss long-term placement issues for the patient, Kath. Kath had ongoing medical problems, including severe arthritis and cancer. The hospice staff expected her to live for some time and, as she was unable to live with her family, a transfer to a suitable nursing home needed to be arranged. I accompanied Felicity as we met first with Kath's family and then had a meeting with Kath, Rob the doctor and Kath's family. Kath made it quite clear she did not want to go to a nursing home but realised she probably did not have any other options. While it would appear to be practical to speak to the family separately from Kath, why were there two meetings and not one? Many of these family meetings are carefully controlled to avoid confrontation and to reach compromises in an efficient manner. In Kath's case, compromises had to be reached through negotiation and prioritisation of needs. While to all appearances Kath had a supportive family, they were not prepared to take her into their home to care for her. In other cases, patients refuse to be cared for by their family, either because they do not want to burden their family or because they do not wish to live with the family for other reasons. The way power is distributed in families is also subject to a great deal of variation and this can complicate the way decisions are made about the patient's treatment and the place of treatment, as the following story illustrates.

Francesa loved her stay of respite in the hospice and was, in the words of one of the nurses, 'stuck to the place, with very little intention of moving'. However, with the pressure for beds for other respite patients, the staff were forced to make provisions for her to return home. There were good reasons for Francesa not wanting to return home. Her husband and son refused to look after her, and expected her to care for them and their home despite her illness. She eventually returned home and, while the community nurses tried to provide support, Francesa's husband was manipulative and demanding. He would organise for a volunteer to sit with her, then decide to stay at home. On other occasions he would leave Francesa unattended for hours at a time. Francesa returned to the inpatient hospice for further respite and I also saw her in another inpatient unit where she spent an extended period of time. These difficult 'family dynamics' continued until the time of her death, and the degree to which she had any control in the quality of her life in the time before her death is questionable. In Francesa's case, the 'family dynamics' were overlaid with cultural values found in the male-dominated society of her birth. Her family had migrated from El Salvador four years previously, and she had very little command of the English language. She was socially isolated and became increasingly reliant on a few kind friends and the institutional supports provided within the health system.

CONCLUSION

In order to understand the experience of terminal illness, we must consider the personal and social worlds of dying people and how they relate to others within these worlds. They are shrinking worlds, contracting into intimate space and time as the terminal illness changes the body and the person. Terminally ill people live until they die, but their living is irretrievably changed as they begin to live their dying. The signs of deterioration are of great importance to the person. This watchfulness gives rise to a state of 'inner time' rather than 'social time' (Melucci 1989, p. 106) as the focus changes from others to self. The self is constructed in such a way that it acknowledges something beyond an intellectualised sphere of understanding. Despite the tendency in Western thought to distinguish between body and mind, flesh and intellect, we long for the opposite. 'People today still spontaneously point to somewhere in the region of their heart when they are asked whereabouts in the body their true self may be found' (Lundin & Akesson 1996, p. 11). It seems, then, that the dying person's body is the entrance to their personal world. When a person begins to die, his or her body is not in harmony with a true personal self or identity. The changing focus of identity shifts that person's ability to relate in an autonomous and deliberate manner.

We must also consider the wider social world of the terminally ill person as that person has acted, and still acts, within the world in socially prescribed ways. Identity changes through terminal illness, but still that identity is imprinted with characteristics determined by gender, ethnicity, social class and age. Terminally ill people's lives, then, are seldom altered 'in radical ways which contradict the usual social positions and expectations they have had as men or women, wealthy or poor, young or old' (Kellehear 1994, p. 184). Their relationships within their close social network also continue, though their existential crises and physical needs heighten bonds and previous tensions. Though we will all die, regardless of our position in society, none of us can be certain about what dying will involve. We are all assailed by the uncertainty associated with disease, its outcomes and treatments. Furthermore, many of us are confronted with uncertainties about the meaning of both life and death, though many still believe in a life after death—whatever this entails. However, 'the lack of a single account of death serves to increase the threat that death poses to the social order' (Edgar 1996, p. 163). Despite the coherence and meaning attributed to human activity, we all inevitably live in fragile personal and social worlds because death remains outside the control of society.

six

Medicine's affair with death

For nearly 200 years, medicine has conducted a complicated affair with death. It was at first halting and flirtatious, an experiment through a period where religion struggled to hold on to and exert power over death. The Enlightenment (the seventeenth and eighteenth centuries in Europe) cast doubt upon the spiritual nature of death's passage and a new modernist period of scientific rationality encouraged medicine's interest in controlling death (Aries 1974; Illich 1976). The desire to control death is fraught with difficulty. For most people, as Nuland suggests in his influential book *How We Die* (1993, p. xv), 'death remains a hidden secret, as eroticized as it is feared'. The startling introduction of various kinds of medical technology which prolong the dying process has not exposed this secrecy and often seems to complicate the dying process by introducing emotionally confronting and ethically difficult problems. Death is awkward, embarrassing and frightening to us all, and medicine has not alleviated our uncertainty, confusion and fear—our inherent fragility in the face of death. This fragility is particularly notable in those who are close to death and reliant upon the science of medicine. The relationship between medicine and death is also fragile. It is just like an illicit romantic affair and is plagued with social, moral, psychological, biological and legal problems.

Anthropological studies have pointed to the striking symbolism of fertility and sexuality which is so frequently found in death rituals. It is notable that these rituals occur after death, for in small-scaled societies people felt they had little control over dying, which often struck swiftly and cruelly and was explained by reference to gods, ancestors and witchcraft. However, the transformation of the living into a dead being, and from there into an ancestor through the 'rite of passage' (Van Gennep 1960), required the cooperative effort of the community. It was essential that the ancestors were benevolent and through their successful intervention they contributed to agricultural production and hunting success and more generally to the fecundity of life. In a more secular setting, contemporary members of society still seek to control the dangerous areas of sex and death. Without both, we are bereft of social relations, yet both have the potential to disrupt not only personal lives but societies as a whole. The improprieties of an American president were disruptive to the functioning of that society just as the unexpected death of an abandoned English princess and her lover inspired a flowering of modern grieving practices.

Medicine, like religion, is a social institution created to help humans deal with important problems, but unlike religion, medicine focuses on the development of technology. In this chapter, I discuss how the development of this technology has created new problems for human society. It is now not so much a problem of how we manage death through medicine or religion, but how we can manage medicine in order to pave the way to a gentler and freer death. Those who practise medicine are constantly confronted with the possibilities and realities of death and with their associated meanings. Yet the dogma of medicine does not explain death beyond the cessation of life and, unlike religion, it does not attempt to give meaning to the finality of death. Alternatively, the institution of medicine manages death principally by preventing it, or at the very least delaying the cessation of life. Yet, while making it difficult for individuals to accept death, medicine has paradoxically helped to provide those individuals with a longer and healthier life in which it is possible to contemplate the inevitability of their demise. On occasion, of course, the life is not necessarily healthier but rather the quality of life is traded off for a longer stay. The affair between medicine and death is a power play, a dance in which every gesture and turn is riddled with ambiguity—for the vast majority of humans really do not want to die, yet all must eventually succumb.

THE ASSOCIATION AND ITS CONSEQUENCES

There is a strong association between death and medicine within contemporary Western societies. Lupton (1994, p. 44) suggests that in the late twentieth century the biological lesion or the positive test result for cancer has replaced the Grim Reaper as the most potent symbol of death. The skeletal figure dressed in black and carrying the scythe was generally kept at bay by living a good life dictated by religious belief. During the period 1650–1850, Protestant ritual and belief, rather than medicine, were closely associated with death in British people's lives (Porter & Porter 1988). Historians Porter and Porter note that, throughout the 200-year period, it was critically important to die the 'good death', yet how one died 'well' changed during that period. Where early in the seventeenth century the good death meant vigilance and preparation to meet a feared God, later in the same century people saw God as a benevolent and forgiving deity. However, by the nineteenth century, hospital foundations had been laid and public health was established. Medicine was on the offensive against disease. Illich (1976, p. 194) argues that during the Enlightenment, doctors established a new power through their claims of influence over death. However, these claims were made regardless of any real proof of ability to influence the dangerous outcomes of sickness.

McKeown (1979) has further argued that the role of medicine in reducing mortality rates, particularly those associated with infectious disease, is debatable. The major influences that have contributed to increased longevity in Western societies are improved public health and, to some extent, improved diet. However, while medicine is not responsible for the major improvements in health over the past two centuries, it has contributed, in a substantial way, to contemporary patterns of longevity and relative health. In the minds of the public, medicine plays a huge part in keeping us all alive, and is constantly linked with combating death. The medicalisation of dying and death is indeed now part of the broader project of the medicalisation of life (Zola 1972; Field 1994). Writing of the North American experience, Kearl (1995, pp. 16–17) extends this medicalisation thesis to an increasing politicalisation of death whereby Americans have 'faith that medical science will provide a cure for anything that ails them'. Medicine is consequently invested with great power, not unlike the military; large numbers of people from all levels of the social hierarchy are absorbed and integrated into medicine's death avoidance project; and matters of death become part of the group's politically structured thought processes. The argument that medicine has assumed great power and is an institution of social control similar to religion or law (Zola 1972) has been very influential in the development of theory in the health social sciences.

These theories of social control have been refined in the work of Foucault (1973, 1989, 1991), who has discussed the way power is dispersed throughout society. Yet dispersed power is also specifically linked to different kinds of knowledges which are used to define people and human behaviour. Medical knowledge, which comes under the rubric of scientific knowledge, is at the top of Foucault's proposed hierarchy of knowledges.

Medicine, therefore, has shaped and limited the possibilities for individual expression (Petersen 1994, p. 6). However, within the discourse of medical knowledge, which includes lay as well as expert opinions, people engage in power relations of domination and resistance. Scientific interpretations of medicine are not always accepted by the lay populace—they are often rejected or modified to suit the needs of the individual (Davis & George 1993, pp. 371–72; Williams & Calnan 1996). Later in this chapter, I will discuss this kind of resistance as it relates to dying, a resistance seen in both the palliative care and euthanasia movements. Medicine also does not simply act as an institution of social control that employs doctors as agents in a quest for powerful knowledge. Medicine's other great and truly wonderful power is its ability, in some instances, to liberate individuals from the devastating effects of disease and pain.

HOW TECHNOLOGY DEFINES THE CAUSES, TIME AND PLACE OF DEATH

Cassell (1975) proposed, some time ago, that within the United States (which may also apply to some degree in other Western societies) there has been a shift in the arena of death from the moral to the technical order. With the increasing reliance on technology, Cassell suggests that people do not expect to die, and look to modern medical centres and hospitals as temples of the technical order. This situation has serious implications for the manner in which people living in contemporary Western societies can expect to die, as articulated by Baume (1993, p. 792), a well-known Australian doctor:

> Our technical successes during the 20th Century have removed many of the straightforward causes of death, so that those remaining are more unpleasant and more undignified, and the events leading up to death are more prolonged. The implications of our therapeutic successes for the provision of sufficient services and care are serious enough, but the implications of great therapeutic advances for our prospects of living and dying well are greater.

The technologically interventionist focus of modern medicine sets contemporary patterns of illness (morbidity) and death (mortality) firmly into the modern way of living. People in the Western industrialised world share similar patterns of mortality and morbidity (Davis & George 1993, pp. 70–74). This means that infant mortality is low, and that people die in older age—men in their mid-seventies and women in their late seventies to early eighties. From 45 years on, the degenerative diseases, such as ischaemic heart disease, cancer, cerebrovascular disease and obstructive airways disease, are the main killers. With these kinds of long-term diseases, there is not only uncertainty in relation to the time it will take to die, there is also uncertainty as to the timing of both biological and social death.

The rise of medical technology in the late 1950s and early 1960s created a new ambiguity about the definition of dying. Gavin (1995) attributes the development of artificial respirators and the ability of doctors to perform organ transplants to an increasing social, moral and legal ambiguity surrounding death. Although it is difficult to establish the timing of death, it is usually considered a biological event, rather than a process of dying which incorporates the social loss of a person. Cassell (1975, p. 45) states that death involves two distinct things: the death of the body and the 'passing' of the person. Medicine focuses on the death of the body, which is strictly monitored by doctors who cast the 'clinical gaze' (Foucault 1973) upon the deteriorating body, determining whether it is fit to salvage. The *process* of dying is ignored and death occurs when the body, or the part of the body which is considered necessary for the life of the body, fails. Thus failure to breathe, heart failure, whole brain and brain stem failure have all been used at different times as a locus to determine biological death.

Experts, most often from the medical establishment, are called upon to define when a death occurs. This is not an easy task, as new technologies which enable resuscitation and life support cast both technical and moral doubt over the timing and the definition of death. There has been a significant critique of any attempt to operationalise death (Veatch 1976; Gavin 1995), but this is usually instigated by those who are interested in the social and ethical aspects of death rather than by the medical establishment as a whole. Notably, it is the medical profession which often has the final say as to the timing of biological death. Gavin (1995, pp. 61–62) suggests that medicine claims the rigorous standards of objectivity found in the natural sciences: 'From this perspective death appears as a problem, a "theoretical entity" or final "disease" that can be precisely defined via operational procedures, and perhaps, as a disease, even ultimately overcome.'

Callahan (1993, p. 61) argues that if death is viewed as a correctable biological deficiency, medicine is then required morally to defeat the disease which causes the death. Yet, if this is the case, the kind of morality called upon to battle the onset of death is couched within the 'value free' ideology so often associated with technical rationality. However, medicalised deaths are not value free. Medicine is value laden, and is, in the words of Good (1994, p. 68), 'a symbolic form through which reality is formulated and organized in a distinctive manner'. Technologically manipulated death is elaborated in radically different forms in the scientifically sophisticated spaces of Japan and North America (Lock 1996), which means that science alone is not responsible for arbitrating on the timing of death. As Lock elaborates in her discussion of death in technological time, the margins between nature and culture are assigned different moral status in the respective dominant ideologies of both cultural spaces. Many of those who practise medicine contribute to the hegemony whereby medicalised death is still considered the norm.

The implications of dying reliant on technology and the therapeutic successes of medicine have meant that most people in contemporary Western societies die in hospital or in other institutional settings like nursing homes. Statistics, which are often difficult to obtain, indicate where people take their last breath, but it is often unclear how long they have been in institutional care. Seale and Cartwright (1994, p. 19) analysed 1987 data which indicated that in England and Wales, 50 per cent of people died in hospitals, 14 per cent died in another institution, 4 per cent died in hospices and 32 per cent died either in their own home or elsewhere. Data from the United States for 1988 show comparable figures; the number of deaths occurring in medical centres was 58.8 per cent, 16.4 per cent of people died in other institutions, and 4.4 per cent were dead on arrival at hospital (Quint Benoliel & Degner 1995, p. 123). Figures for the place of death in Australia are not routinely collected, but unpublished data accessed through hospital coding systems indicate that in Western Australia in 1995, of the 10 355 people who died, approximately 71 per cent did so in hospitals, nursing homes or hospices; 22 per cent died at home; and 7 per cent died elsewhere (Australian Bureau of Statistics 1997).

The reason people mostly die in institutional care can be partially explained by the increase in chronic illnesses which often necessitate medical care. However, these chronic illnesses are in some senses bolstered by the technological focus of medicine. In the twentieth century, hospital services have been shaped by the growing influence of the biomedical model of disease, adopting highly specialised and technical procedures as the dominant form of therapy (Quint Benoliel & Degner 1995, p. 124). With such a curative focus, hospitals are not always the best place for terminally ill people to spend their last hours, days or weeks. Yet the hospital has become an institution for dying which has cultural significance for many people. Responsibility for the management of dying has shifted from the family to the medical and nursing experts who work in hospitals, where the use of technology is routinised. Koenig (1988, p. 469) suggests that the highly routinised nature of medicine is not surprising, as 'illness is by its very nature chaotic and unpredictable' and habitualisation makes it unnecessary for each situation to be defined anew. The use of technology ironically offers some kind of clinical assurance, when death is, in fact—like illness—chaotically social and personal. Technology offers no real answers to the pain of leaving others behind.

WALKING ON WATER AS WELL?

Not all medical practitioners subscribe to the dominant belief that medicine should be used to combat dying, and many appear disillusioned with their colleagues who engage in salvational methods. One of the doctors whom I have worked with commented angrily that a professor of surgery he had encountered not only had a 'distorted view of palliative care' but that he had 'taken up walking on water as well'. Why is it that many doctors take on this god-like role? There is no straightforward answer to this question but it does direct our attention to the uncertainty that is still associated with dying and death, regardless of the wonders of technology. Stripped of the safeguards accorded by religion and ritual, members of Western societies and their 'priests in white coats' have tended to look to medicine to provide the salvation once promised by the church. Good (1994, p. 70) proposes that medicine responds to the materialist individualism in 'modern societies' and is at the core of the quest to understand, transform and transcend suffering and achieve salvation. This is part of what Geertz (1988, p. 146) has called 'a salvational belief in the powers of science'. Medicine both reinforces and proposes technological mastery over ultimate death, and health replaces salvation, as Foucault wrote in *The Birth of the Clinic* (1973, p. 198):

> Medicine offers modern man the obstinate, yet reassuring face of his finitude; in it, death is endlessly repeated, but it is also exorcised; and although it ceaselessly reminds man of the limit that he bears within him, it also speaks to him of that technical world that is the armed, positive, full form of his finitude.

SINKING AND SWIMMING IN THE POOL OF DEATH

Many medical practitioners, when confronted with the huge and bottomless pool of death, may attempt to walk on water but begin to sink only to learn in time to swim. In the book *How We Die*, Dr Sherwin Nuland explains this process. In a candid confessional chapter entitled 'Lessons I Have Learned', Nuland (1993) says 'one of the worst errors that can be made during terminal illness' is that of not admitting to the painful truth, but deciding instead to avoid a final sharing that may have added dignity to the 'anguishing fact of death' (1993 p. 244). Nuland suggests that the quest of every doctor in approaching serious disease is to diagnose and carry out a cure. He calls this 'The Riddle' and argues that doctors at times convince their patients to undergo tests and treatments that go beyond reason, for ultimately The Riddle must often remain unsolved (1993, p. 248). Miss Welch, a 92-year-old patient of

Nuland's, was cajoled into surgery she did not want. He admits the surgery was ill-advised and that the patient was made angry by his well-intentioned deception. 'I had won out over The Riddle but lost the greater battle of humane patient care' (1993, p.252). Nuland learns from his mistakes and begins to swim in the treacherous waters though, like many of his colleagues, he suggests he has broken the law to ease a patient's going. It is not simply a matter of learning to swim, for sometimes a struggle ensues where one doctor stays afloat by pushing both the patient and other health professionals under. In the following example, the patient's interests are sacrificed in an undignified power play. The story has been pieced together from the accounts of members of a multidisciplinary team of palliative care professionals who cared for the patient. Mr Johnson, a 76-year-old man, was (according to the team) suffering from cancer. Significant medical and surgical investigations had not revealed the primary site of the cancer and the surgeon, Professor Broderick, had told the family that Mr Johnson should recover. John, one of the team doctors, said: 'Typical Prof Broderick . . . he's [the patient] got leaking problems, a faecal leak, but he *hasn't* got cancer.' John had heard that Professor Broderick had told the hospital staff where Mr Johnson was being treated that 'his patient' was not a suitable candidate for palliative care. He told the hospital nurses to remove the morphine pump that had been previously established by a visiting palliative care consultant who had been called in to manage Mr Johnson's pain. When Mr Johnson was due to go home for the weekend, the nurses on the ward talked the resident doctor into referring the patient to the palliative care home service.

The palliative care team doctors claimed that Mr Johnson would not have survived that weekend without their medical input. When Professor Broderick heard of the arrangements, he subsequently called Mr Johnson's family and suggested that they receive support from the general district nursing service and not the palliative care service. The family became confused and felt unable to manage. How were they to interpret the differing messages that they were receiving about Mr Johnson's condition? Should they prepare for his death or encourage him to battle on, which was not an easy task considering his weakened condition. Mr Johnson was subsequently readmitted to hospital for continuing surgical and medical treatment. He did not leave the hospital ward and died only weeks later.

Mr Johnson's dying and death was, despite the input of the palliative care services, a mismanaged affair. Mr Johnson and his family did not appear to have a substantial degree of control in deciding the course of the illness, the treatment, or the manner of dying and death. The palliative care team were frustrated and concerned that, despite continuing medical treatment, Mr Johnson remained in pain. He also was unaware of his terminal state because one doctor was more concerned with solving 'The Riddle' than with allowing Mr Johnson and his family to spend what time remained together unencumbered by invasive procedures.

Place and time play a significant part in the way in which the power to make decisions about the future is appropriated from the patient and family by the surgeon. Frankenberg (1992, p. 25), commenting on the cultural performance of sickness within a biomedical framework, notes the disruption of social and temporal mechanisms which are used to control relationships of nature and culture: '[I]n order to maintain social order and restore natural order, patients are removed from their normal temporalities to a space where the time view of others can be imposed upon them.' Though this is an integral part of what Frankenberg calls the '*modus operandi* of biomedicine' it has particular implications for the dying patient. The patient, Mr Johnson, was monitored within the hospital and subjected to the institution's temporal peculiarities—routines took precedence over, and ultimately distorted, Mr Johnson's own dying trajectory. Within the hierarchy of the medical structure, the surgeon held the power and the family were inclined to accept his advice; within the realm of the hospital it seems that it did not occur to the patient and the family that they may have other options. Within this realm, Mr Johnson's death is defined as a biological failure occurring at a precise time. This is principally because the surgeon, who assumed the responsibility and associated power, refused to acknowledge that Mr Johnson was dying. Muller and Koenig (1988, p. 351) note:

> [I]f patients are not defined as dying until they are very close to physiological death, they are not treated as dying persons and consequently may receive, in the attempt to 'save' them, the very intensive technological interventions that conjure up frightening images of horrible, machine-dependent deaths.

Not only will patients in this situation be subject to machine-dependent deaths, they may not be given the opportunity to discuss their approaching death. The lack of open discussion about death denies the patient and their family the opportunity to make final preparations, resolve their differences and say their farewells.

RESISTING THE MEDICALISATION OF DYING AND DEATH

Palliative care has the potential to disrupt the medicalisation of death, but this is often hampered, as illustrated in the case of Mr Johnson. In other cases, many patients receive wonderful care from palliative care teams and die in the manner they wish—at home with their families, or at least surrounded by the people they love in a nurturing environment.

Elsewhere in this book I have discussed how the birth of the hospice movement, as part of a broader death awareness movement, challenged the role of medicine in the care of terminally ill people. A great deal has been achieved in holding back invasive kinds of technology that can turn dying into a clinical nightmare. However, there are paradoxical tensions even within palliative care that are reflective of the ambivalent relationship between medicine and death, as I discuss in Chapter 10. The practitioners of this unique form of care come 'armed' with the technology aimed to prevent death, hoping to reinterpret the salvational view of science. Medicine will not then 'save' terminally ill people from death, but ease them gently towards their end. It is important to note that medicine acts as the key organising symbol within the practice of palliative care. Medicine, therefore, is deeply implicated in the processes by which the care is organised in these services.

Medicine, while framed within a scientific rationalist discourse, is often more contradictory and haphazard than neatly reductive and reflective of an idealised biomedical model. This often appears to be the case in terminal care, where the human elements of suffering cast clinical, social, existential and moral uncertainties upon the interactions between patients and health professionals. Nevertheless, despite a growing transformation of the traditional biomedical approach cultivated by dissatisfaction from both within and outside the profession of medicine, the power of medicine as a legitimate response to suffering is tangible and ever-present within contemporary society. Patterns of medical dominance are evident even within the palliative care community, as I illustrate more fully in Chapter 10. Other attempts to make sense of this increasingly difficult area of terminal care come from geriatricians who propose the use of 'living wills' or 'health care directives' (Molloy & Clarnette 1993; Waddell et al. 1997). These well-intentioned suggestions which seek to empower patients, however, are often fraught with legal and practical difficulties.

Given the obvious difficulties associated with dealing with medicine from within the culture itself, it may be that contemporary societies need to deal with the problems associated with dying in other ways. These kinds of attempts to deal with the medicalisation of death have been more drastic and have involved impassioned non-medical individuals, community groups and parliamentarians, as well as select members of the medical profession who often appear as renegade doctors. Some years ago I unwrapped the plastic wrapper from a book marked candidly with a Category One 'R', meaning it was restricted and not available to persons under eighteen years. In this simple act of opening the controversial book entitled *Final Exit* (Humphry 1991), I was reminded of how Gorer (1955) had railed against the 'pornography of death'. However, in the case of Humphry's book, it is not death that is considered restricted in a manner usually reserved for blatantly eroticised and unusual sex, but the manner to achieve death. In *Final Exit*, Humphry outlines the practicalities of self-deliverance and assisted suicide for the dying. The book was designed, in the absence of voluntary euthanasia legislation, to provide information to terminally ill people which would enable them to decide how, and when to die.

Since that time, Australia has engaged in a unique but short-lived social experiment in euthanasia. The Northern Territory of Australia passed legislation in 1996 (Rose 1997; Quirk 1998) allowing euthanasia, but this was subsequently overturned in the Senate. However, the provisions associated with the legislation and the practicalities involved meant that that only a few people took advantage of the legislation. Nevertheless, the topic was definitely on the agenda for public discussion, as I discuss in Chapter 2, and the topic continues to be aired by the media when community groups of avid campaigners recharge the debate. This debate divides the community, though public support of voluntary euthanasia for terminally ill people is consistently cited at approximately 60–70 per cent (Roy Morgan Research Centre 1996). Medical professionals are also divided, as I discuss in Chapter 2. A recent survey showed that end-of-life treatment is 'significantly determined by an array of individual characteristics of the doctor and not solely by the nature of the medical problem' (Waddell et al. 1996, p. 540). While individual characteristics do play a large part, so do the meanings associated with being a doctor. These meanings are complex and often contradictory, for doctors are called on to be compassionate and caring, but they are also socialised into the paternalistic and dominant roles the profession demands (Willis 1983; Freidson 1970a).

CONCLUSION

Medicine's affair with death is truly complicated. In the book *Dancing With Mister D* (Keizer 1996) based on Dr Bert Keizer's experiences in a nursing home in Amsterdam, Keizer says: 'Nobody delivers himself on to this planet as nobody dies himself off it. So dying is hard to define. The most satisfactory idea is that of a struggle near the exit after which you are let through' (1996, p. 17). The struggle may relate to the fact that it is difficult to give up life, but it also alludes to the struggle with the medical profession who closely monitor the exit. The cover of this book uses an etching by Ivo Saliger (1921) which depicts an evocative *ménage à trois*. In the foreground a naked woman clings to a white-robed doctor, but is at the same time embraced lovingly by the skeletal figure of death. In the background framed by opulent red velvet and gold cord is a glass-panelled door with the lettering 'WAY OUT'. The woman could be any patient, but the enduring relationship here is between the dominant males who struggle in a last dance with the passive dying patient. Not surprisingly, the woman's face is obscured as the doctor and death-like figure tentatively touch in their struggle to claim her.

Keizer reminds his readers that medicine is not simply the product of 150 years of scientific endeavour, but also bears the heritage of 15 000 years where 'the doctor performed as priest, soothsayer, magician, prophet and wholesale dealer' (1996, p. 69). It is this combination of science, ritual and magic which empowers doctors to dance with death. Deathbed technology has become a scientific façade which covers over the existential questions which continue to plague us as humans. And what is the doctor to do when, like Keizer, he or she is confronted with a patient who knows the truth:

> He looks away from me . . . 'And now I am certain that I'm dying.' He tells me how terrible it is to know that. 'Can I do anything for you? Shall I call a priest?' 'No.' Why do I sound so inadequate, as if I have said, 'Would you like a cup of coffee or something?' (1996, p. 9)

There is a great deal of uncertainty associated with dying, and it seems the doctor maybe should, at times, embrace rather than reject inadequacy. There simply are no easy answers and the affair remains complicated by social, moral, psychological, biological and legal problems which take death away from the realm of medicine and place it firmly in the public view.

seven

Speaking the 'truth' about dying

Many people find it uncomfortable to discuss issues relating to dying and death, yet death is an ever-present reality which is not totally ignored, but pushed to the back of our minds while we go about the business of daily living. On occasion we are forced to think about dying and this is most poignantly brought to the foreground of our thoughts through the news of a life-threatening illness. This news, usually delivered in the doctor's office, brutally interrupts everyday life, but does it encourage open discussion about dying and death? We can only address this question and the other complex issues that surround truth-telling and open discussion about dying and death through detailed research and social comment. In this chapter, I use some of my research in this area (described in Chapter 1) to suggest that many people in Western societies are strong and often outspoken when it comes to formulating opinions about the role of the doctor in truth-telling about terminal illness. Outspoken people are often removed from the reality of death and when placed in the vulnerable position of having received a life-threatening diagnosis or terminal prognosis, their opinions can change. A common strategy for coping, adopted by terminally ill people and their families from various cultural backgrounds, is to shore up the fragile life with silence and pretence. Another strategy is to engage in a haphazard style of communication, which swings between silence and acceptance, not just on a daily basis, but within the same conversation. However, there are also those brave individuals who expose their fragility and fear, and some also who embrace death openly as a welcome release from illness and exhaustion.

This chapter considers the role of the health professional, particularly the doctor, in the process of delivering the 'bad news' and encouraging family discussion about approaching death. As death has become increasingly associated with medicine, as I argue in Chapter 6, the requirement that the doctor deliver correct and reliable information to the patient has changed. From an initial lack of concern for informing the patient, the doctor now feels obliged, both ethically and legally, to deliver the diagnosis and prognosis. This requirement has contributed a burden, which often weighs heavily upon both the individual doctor and the profession. For many doctors, the ideal and the reality force them into a double bind. No doubt the correct information provides opportunities for the patient to engage in autonomous decision-making, but what if the patient is elderly, demented, sedated or of non-English speaking background? The principle of autonomy gives precedence to the individual, but where does the family fit into the picture? Is the family indeed present, as it is so often now the case that the 'family' is redefined by the individual to exclude some and include others who share intimacy but not biology. Other families live at a distance, and in other cases cultural beliefs contribute to a protectiveness which shelters the ill person from damaging news about approaching death. There are no simple answers, but perhaps there are lessons to be learned from the stories of patients, their families and their health professional carers.

DISCUSSIONS SURROUNDING DYING AND DEATH

It is not unusual to hear the comment that death is a 'taboo' topic. Aries (1974, 1981) has explored the denial of death thesis in detail, suggesting that the attitude of Western societies towards death is characterised by fear and shame. Gorer's (1965) work, written not long after World War II, was also very influential in establishing the denial theme and proposed that death had replaced sex as the taboo topic in contemporary societies. The idea that death is a taboo topic is now a somewhat outdated notion. Both Kellehear (1984, 1996) and Walter (1991) have suggested that people do not refuse to speak about death, they simply become embarrassed by the topic because it does not seem appropriate in polite conversation. This embarrassment is particularly painful when we search for words at the bedside of a terminally ill family member or friend. Elias (1985, p. 23), in his book *The Loneliness of Dying*, notes 'a peculiar embarrassment felt by the living in the presence of dying people. They often do not know what to say. The range of words available for use in this situation is relatively narrow.' Discussions about dying and death have changed considerably over the past 40 years. In the context of present times, dying and death have become topics that many people do wish to discuss and this is demonstrated daily in the media and in 'ordinary' conversations. As a researcher in the area of dying and death, I often engage in conversations with people who are not averse to discussing dying and death in social encounters, as well as in academic and clinical settings. Euthanasia, particularly, has become a topic of enormous social interest since the enactment (1996) and subsequent overturning of legislation (1997) in the Northern Territory of Australia (Rose 1997; Quirk 1998).

The reason why people have become more prepared to challenge the supposedly 'taboo' topic of death needs to be seen in the context of what has been termed the 'death awareness' movement (Metcalf & Huntington 1991, p. 25). Prominent in this movement—which encouraged open discussion about dying and death—were Kubler-Ross (1969), who proposed a stage theory of death acceptance, and Saunders, who is credited as the founder of the modern hospice movement. By tracing the theoretical arguments of many prominent scholars (Blauner 1966; Aries 1974, 1981; Cassell 1975; Illich 1976; Elias 1985; Bauman 1992), we can see that this 'new' awareness of dying and death arose during the 1960s. Since then it has grown in response to the modern Western cultural shift towards institutionalised, secularised and medicalised deaths. Contemporary responses to dying and death seem to indicate that Western societies are undergoing a period of transition where the topic of dying and death is increasingly claimed as a public issue. This is evidenced in the increasing acceptance of palliative care, as well as in the growing voluntary euthanasia lobby. However, dying and death are still mostly removed from the business of daily life, relegated to the hospital ward and placed in the hands of strangers (McNamara et al. 1994; McNamara et al. 1995). As I have already indicated, despite this more public acceptance of discussions about death, truth-telling and open discussion surrounding dying and death are not straightforward matters. I will explore many of the problems associated with this kind of discussion later in the chapter. The next section, however, provides some analytical comment on an Australian survey that I conducted with Charles Waddell (1997) in order to demonstrate the general public's acceptance of more open discussion about death.

WOULD YOU WANT TO KNOW THE TRUTH?

In this survey about end-of-life decision-making, Anglo and Chinese Australians were asked how favourable they were to being told they had a terminal or life-threatening illness. Another question addressed the issue of how favourable they were to a close relative or loved one being told of a terminal or life-threatening illness. Patterns of belief are located within this data, which reveal that, rather than ignoring the possibility of terminal illness and death, most people have developed carefully thought-out positions about whether they would want to know the truth. However, there are differences between the way that Anglo and Chinese Australians think about truth-telling issues, which indicate that cultural belief underlies decision-making when faced with death. Whereas aspects of age, gender, level of education, religious belief and perceived quality of life and health did not differ in a statistically significant way, we did find that significantly fewer Chinese Australians than Anglo Australians desired to be told the truth about terminal illness.

Most doctors in Western countries have been disclosing the truth about cancer and other terminal illnesses to their patients for many years (Good et al. 1990; Thomsen et al. 1993). Accordingly, most people want to be told the truth about their diagnosis (Ashby & Wakefield 1993). The survey we conducted confirms this, with 95 per cent of Anglo Australians and 86 per cent of Chinese Australians wishing to be told the truth about their terminal or life-threatening illness. While significantly fewer Chinese Australians than Anglo Australians desire truth-telling, a large proportion do want to be told. Conversely, there are some people from both cultural backgrounds who do not wish to be told the truth. It is interesting that most Chinese Australians in the study wished to be told the truth about their own diagnosis. However, 63 per cent of the Chinese Australian respondents would not want their ill relative to be told the truth about a terminal or life-threatening illness. Many Chinese Australian families feel it is their duty to protect their family and loved ones from the truth and this is something I have confirmed in interviews with ethnic Chinese people. However, the patients themselves may be likely to want to know the truth.

It is difficult for medical practitioners to determine the wishes of the individual and the family, particularly in the sensitive area of terminal illness (Mitchell 1998). The wishes of the individual may conflict with those of the family, whether this is in relation to disclosure of diagnosis or the chosen direction of treatment options. While knowledge of the patient's cultural background cannot relieve the practitioner of the ethical obligation to conduct a discussion about the illness, it will help them to structure the discussion in the appropriate manner. These issues become even more complex when they are taken out of a hypothetical context presented in the form of a survey and viewed from the perspective of terminally ill patients and their family members. As cultural background appears so central to our beliefs about dying and death, the following discussion focuses on the cultural beliefs of people of both Anglo and non-English speaking background. Cultural expression seems nowhere more salient than at the final rite of passage (Metcalf & Huntington 1991), for it seems that, in the process of dying, people hold on to the beliefs and behaviours which contribute to their increasingly fragile sense of identity.

TRUTH-TELLING ABOUT CANCER AND DEATH IN A MULTICULTURAL CONTEXT

Truth-telling about terminal illness is mostly associated with the diagnosis of cancer, and I have discussed the association between cancer and death in Chapter 3. The diagnosis of cancer introduces the threat of death in the mind of the patient; discussion surrounding cancer is therefore difficult for both the patient and the health professional. Open discussion about cancer and death is difficult in many health care settings and, indeed, in many countries. For example, in Japan, Italy, Greece and India, naming the cancer diagnosis instils such fear that it may lead to immediate 'social death' (Good et al. 1990; Gordon 1990). Informing the patient about his or her cancer diagnosis has only become practice in countries like Britain and Australia in the past ten to fifteen years (Field 1989; Hunt 1994). Through the introduction of such open discussion in these countries, there has been a growing acceptance amongst the medical community that providing correct information to patients improves their autonomy (Hunt 1994).

In a study carried out with colleagues on the nature of culturally appropriate palliative care (McNamara et al. 1998), the majority of terminally ill people interviewed knew their diagnosis of cancer. Fifty-three people from 22 different ethnic backgrounds, including Anglo Australian, were interviewed. These people were either terminally ill themselves or were a family member of a terminally ill person. Of those who were of non-English speaking background, most had been in Australia for some time (an average of 31 years) and could speak English. Most people used the word 'cancer'; however, four of the Italian-born people and five of the people born in other European countries avoided using the term. These people tended to explain their illness in terms of 'a growth' or 'a stomach problem'. Maria, an Italian-born bereaved woman, explained that the doctor insisted on telling her Italian-born husband that he had cancer, but from that time on they did not discuss it.

All this time, I never talked to him—to ask why—he couldn't talk about it . . . why do you have to talk about the end of life, when the time comes it does . . . it's better to pass away than to know exactly what the problem is, to say something 'Oh it'll be alright' because once you tell them 'You've got cancer' that is the death sentence.

Italian-born family members appear to be protective towards the terminally ill person and often attempt to shield them from 'bad news'—and a diagnosis of cancer is definitely 'bad news'.

In another interview, an Italian-born bereaved woman and her Australian-born daughter discussed how their deceased loved one had never once discussed dying, but the daughter commented: 'I suppose we wouldn't let him, would we mum?' However, individuals varied in their approaches to discussing the diagnosis and prognosis. Enzo, an Italian-born man, confided that when he had fallen and had a stroke a few mornings before the interview, he wished he had died. He had requested euthanasia and saw no reason to go on living. It is notable, though, that Enzo did not have a family in Australia, nor close family in Italy, and his wish to die and manner of communicating his wishes may have been different if there had been family members to protect him. Another Italian man had a very depressed demeanour and expressed absolute hopelessness: he was badly cared for and bullied by his wife, who freely discussed his 'cancer' in his presence. Families of mixed ethnicity may also adopt cultural practices associated with one culture. Shirley, an Anglo Australian-born terminally ill woman, was married to an Italian man and both he and their children were present for part of the interview. Shirley later confided privately that she knew she was dying, but could not discuss this with her family as they wanted her to be positive and to 'go on living'. Shirley died a week after the interview.

People from various Asian backgrounds also express a reluctance to discuss dying with their terminally ill family members, as Frankie—a bereaved ethnic Chinese man, a nurse by occupation and originally from Hong Kong—explained:

> Oh yes. She probably knew she was dying but the Chinese culture doesn't like to talk [about] this topic. She obviously accepts death, she's got a terminal illness—'I won't live long'—she always expressed that . . . but I think if she raise up this question too often or if I raise up this question too often the relationship would be upset. That is why we don't talk about it.

When asked if he talked about cancer with his mother, Frankie responded:

> I try not to but I cannot avoid to use this term because she overheard what the doctors say. She understand what they say. I try to cover it up—but I can't. She is very sensible . . . I feel sorry she find out because I suspect that that generation does not accept these things, not accept the death.

It appears that many non-English speaking patients prefer their families to receive and manage information for them and many members prefer to do so, a finding confirmed in other empirical research in this area (Huang et al. 1999; Mitchell 1998; Frank et al. 1998; Gordon & Paci 1997; Good et al. 1993).

However, it would be simplistic to apply rules about truth-telling too broadly, and the family and their health professional carers must negotiate each situation as it arises. Anh, a Vietnamese-born man who was part of a family caring for his elderly mother who did not speak English, said it was his duty to protect his mother from the knowledge that she had cancer. Anh explained: 'It is not the Asian way to burden the elderly with such bad news.' However, further discussion demonstrated that this general rule is modified in certain circumstances. Once Anh's mother had returned to Vietnam to spend time with her relatives there, they would let her know that this would be her 'final time' and allow her to decide where she would spend her last days. Anh, at 44 years of age, said that if he were diagnosed with a terminal illness he would want to know so he could settle his affairs, a sentiment expressed by a significant number of younger Chinese Australians in the survey data discussed above (Waddell & McNamara 1997). Asian-born terminally ill people who were in a relatively younger age range expressed a greater knowledge about their cancer and a greater wish for autonomy. Moi, a 42-year-old Chinese Malaysian woman, had suffered with stomach cancer for two years. She believed strongly that she had lived a good life and was pleased that she had outlived the six to twelve months the doctors had told her she had left. Moi laughed throughout the interview and displayed extraordinary courage, saying: 'What will be, will be—I like to live, but I probably won't.' Her elderly, non-English speaking parents cared for Moi and she mentioned that she did not discuss the nature of her illness with her parents.

Of all the participants who were terminally ill, just over half talked about dying and most other patients expressed uncertainty about the future. These patterns were not specific to any cultural group and the findings of this particular study should send a strong message to health practitioners who associate certain behaviours with particular cultural groups. An oncologist I interviewed through the course of my ethnographic fieldwork asserted that:

Multicultural Australia makes practising oncology a minefield because you never know what to say to the next patient that comes in . . . I simply do not have enough chairs in my office for all of the Asian families . . . they are likely to bring in up to sixteen different people and none of them wants to speak about the 'cancer'.

Other research I have conducted (McNamara et al. 1997) demonstrates that palliative care practitioners feel most uncomfortable with people of Asian background. However, the interview material discussed here reveals that a large group of people, regardless of cultural background, talk about their prognosis or eventual death, but certain families have particular wishes which are partly determined by cultural background and this needs to be understood.

Information gathered from the Anglo Australian participants in the study also demonstrates the dangers of stereotyping behaviours by cultural background. While most of the Anglo Australian participants appeared better informed about their illness and prognosis, not all spoke openly about their dying and many were confused about their treatments. Harry, a 72-year-old man with prostate cancer, like many people of his generation, did not discuss his worsening condition but sought to 'battle on'. He also did not criticise the kind of medical care he received. Harry told of how he heard the news of his orchidectomy (removal of the testicles) not from the surgeon he had seen on several occasions, but from the anaesthetist who was preparing him for the operation which was to follow in a matter of minutes. Harry continued to have great faith in medical science, which he believed would provide the means for him to continue living. Perhaps the surgeon had informed Harry of the proposed treatment in what he thought was an appropriate manner, but the lesson to be learned here is that good communication rests on what is heard and understood, not on what is told.

THE ROLE OF THE HEALTH PROFESSIONAL IN TRUTH-TELLING

All health professionals who work with terminally ill people are confronted with a 'rumpled reality' of moral decision-making (Muller 1994, p. 454). This means that there are no ready answers to the difficult questions that patients may ask, but rather an array of problematic situations that are responded to in a number of ways. As Muller (1994) notes, we must give careful scrutiny to the political, institutional and sociocultural factors that lead to the context in which ethical dilemmas appear. These ethical dilemmas seem most pertinent to doctors, for 'normally the decision whether or not to disclose "bad news", especially a terminal prognosis, is controlled by doctors' (Field 1989, p. 7). The contemporary trend to disclose the terminal diagnosis to the patient and, in some cases, to continue discussions about the prognosis must therefore be seen against a backdrop of changes in the medical profession and the broader society. Doctors are now more often called to account for the status and power accorded to them, and the public display an increasing disillusionment with scientific medicine (Lupton 1994). Cultural pluralism evident in Western societies also necessitates multiple versions of appropriate action. I have already discussed many examples of this cultural pluralism in the stories of patients and their families who grapple with versions of the 'truth' about dying. How, then, should health professionals respond to the process of disclosing terminal diagnosis and prognosis?

Perhaps the most useful way of approaching this problem is to reflect upon present practice and to recognise the culturally constituted nature of bioethical and day-to-day decision-making. What cultural assumptions lie behind the decision to disclose or to withhold information about terminal illness? From my many discussions with health professionals, I see a genuine interest in empowering patients and their families to make decisions for themselves. This interest is framed within a broader discourse of individual human rights, yet in practice many of the decisions and discussions fall into a 'grey' area of uncertainty. An example of this kind of uncertainty can be seen in the disclosure norms evident in a palliative care service I have observed in the course of my research. Disclosure norms are the conventions which exist concerning the type of information given to a patient and which ultimately establish predispositions towards action (Field 1989, p. 126). Where disclosure norms are unclear and are not shared by health professionals, uncertainty pervades interactions between patients and staff. Formalised palliative care objectives do not state disclosure norms regarding impending death; rather, they stress the importance of patient autonomy and respect for the rights of individuals (Finlay 1996). However, the concepts of patient autonomy and individual rights can be interpreted differently by health professionals and also mediated by the professional's own level of comfort in discussing difficult issues.

During my research I spoke with Bert, a chaplain who had done temporary work in inpatient hospices over a number of years. Bert has an academic interest in what he calls 'caring until death' and believes that the hospice was originally considered a 'terminus'. More recently, he believes, hospice and palliative care has been reformulated as a way of getting terminally ill people well enough to go home. Bert believed that this has changed the nature of spiritual care in hospices:

> People once knew why they were coming to [the] hospice—to die—this made ministry very specific. There now seems to be a lot more indecision . . . I wander around here and one minute I'm talking to an atheist and the next a Christian. There is indecisiveness about whether or not to discuss preparation for death.

Other health professionals assume patients understand what hospice means. I asked Elsie whether she believed patients knew that they had a terminal illness when they came to the inpatient hospice. She replied:

'If they come in here, how could they not know? They might not talk about it, but they have to know. It is a hospice after all.'

Terminally ill people who are cared for in their own homes may think differently, and as the following example shows, the health professionals may prefer to engage in open discussion with patients but are thwarted in their efforts. Joyce, a nurse who I have worked with, talked in a team meeting about one of the patients, Mr Gordon, who insisted on calling 'his problem' emphysema:

> I tried to tell him it was cancer but he wouldn't listen, just kept asking for oxygen and there were three people puffing away like chimneys in the little flat . . . he's not a well chap, he's all done . . . I don't know if the family know. Perhaps they should be told so they can get his affairs in order. I won't be the one to tell them though.

Brian, the doctor who had been treating Mr Gordon, asserted that the patient had been told about his prognosis, to which Joyce replied: 'Do we give it one more shot then?' Brian avoided this question and began to discuss the weakness in Mr Gordon's hand, commenting on how it was an interesting medical problem and one similar to another patient he had seen recently. Joyce brought the subject back to the 'prognosis' problem again and pressed the doctor to do something more. Brian sighed and said he would 'Go through the rellies' which meant he would speak to the family and ask for their help. Joyce, who had clearly set herself up as 'devil's advocate', then asked: 'And what if they say, but he's only got emphysema doctor?' Brian replied: 'Well I'll just wait and see then—at the end of the day, it hasn't got a lot to do with me has it?'

Even when communication between dying patients and health professionals is open, many health professionals still find it difficult to discuss impending death, as this example, taken from an interview with Mandy, illustrates:

> People accept death a lot easier if they're not looking for every crisis around the corner . . . I'm not into forcing knowledge on people. It's bad enough having cancer without having to talk about it as well. I guess that's the down side of counselling.

Another nurse, Margaret, said:

> It's cruel to tell people they are going to die. They are going to have the same problems whether you intervene or not. How can you tell anyone the truth . . . about what's really imponderable?

Yet there are also many health professionals who engage in lengthy, intimate and difficult conversations with distraught patients and their families, as Tom's comments reflect:

You have to understand this is not an event like an ingrown toenail or appendicitis where you get better and go home. This is about a life ending and the hardest thing for a palliative care doctor is learning to do nothing, to actually stop acting. It's the exact opposite to what we are taught, but on many occasions that is what you have to do. You have to just sit and relate to the person as another person, at a deep level.

By examining the day-to-day interactions between patients, their families and the health professionals who care for them, we can see the complexity of ethical issues in terminal illness. Truth-telling, or the disclosure of diagnosis and prognosis, is situated in a moral discourse employed by people themselves, rather than in the language of the bioethicist. The moral discourse of the health professionals I have interviewed and observed is rooted in a profound respect for the person, but is also overlaid by professional obligations and personal prejudices and skills. Achieving a balance between the rights of the person and professional ethics may appear difficult enough, yet perhaps the initial step may be to examine one's own fears about dying and death. This highly personal strategy focuses on the fragility of our own lives in the face of death. A second strategy requires the health professional to consider the nature of the relationship between the patient and their family and the health professional. Finlay (1996, p. 65) suggests that the relationship between the clinician and the patient 'can only function as a support relationship if it is founded on trust'. Trust in itself is a fragile thing, but importantly it is also a state of comfort built over time. It seems, then, that the responsibility to deliver the truth entails more than the brutal facts, but an understanding of levels of truth and the willingness and capability to accept truth. Most importantly, we can gather from Finlay's suggestion that the social relationship between the patient and the health professional lies at the heart of the matter.

CONCLUSION

There are many good reasons for telling and accepting the truth, as the following quote from Parkes (1978, p. 53) demonstrates:

If only the patient and the family can be helped to share the truth instead of avoiding it, the general level of tension will often be reduced and the need for drugs to reduce emotional tension artificially will diminish. Unfortunately, doctors and nurses usually find it easier to administer the drugs than to take the time to talk with patients and family members in the hope of resolving rather than repressing their problems.

However, the truth is frightening for the patients and their family. It signals both finality and uncertainty and for these reasons many people touched by the process of terminal illness are confused and non-compliant. The truth is also frightening for the health professional because it signals the emotionally hard labour (James 1989) of talking to people who are overwhelmed by grief, and often engaged in the coping strategy of pretence. It is also worth remembering that it is the health professional who, in many senses, controls the power of scientific knowledge about dying. 'Whatever professionals do or do not do, it is unlikely to be challenged by patients who are ill and therefore preoccupied and usually lacking in confidence' (Young & Cullen 1996, p. 113).

Despite these general observations, we must acknowledge the level of Anglo-centrism they assume. Therapy that involves talking about highly personal issues is common to Western psychiatry and clinical psychology, and those of us who come from this tradition are accustomed to 'talking cures' (Anderson 1996, p. 365). The examples I have discussed in this chapter illustrate that, for many people from non-English speaking backgrounds, 'talking cures' may be culturally inappropriate. Patient autonomy and the ethical imperative to inform the patient, while highly valued in Western cultures, may also be limited when viewed in a cross-cultural context. People from an Anglo-centric background may also be averse to open discussion relating to dying and death. The survey data I have discussed confirm that most people would want to know if they were diagnosed with a terminal illness. Yet the qualitative data I have presented also show that the behaviours of terminally ill patients and their families sometimes contradict this premise. Social relationships, therefore, 'may present an equally and sometimes more compelling framework for bioethics than individual rights' (Frank et al. 1998). By focusing on social relationships, then, we can acknowledge the broader context and the complexity of the interactions that happen in health care settings and in the homes of terminally ill people.

eight

Patient autonomy and professional control

In this chapter, I look at two important issues that have been topical in the care of terminally ill people but also relevant to the broader context of contemporary health care. Patient autonomy and professional control are contentious issues in health care and one is often contrasted with the other as if the two were mutually exclusive. In fact, both are negotiated within complex situational settings. Patient autonomy is contingent on many factors that lie outside the patient's control, and professional control is subject as much to the individual doctor's beliefs as it is to the medical profession's directives (Waddell et al. 1996). Ethical decision-making at the end of life is set within what Kleinman (1992, pp. 128–9) calls 'local worlds', where actions have cultural, political, economic, institutional and social relational sources and consequences. These local worlds are also moral worlds where people recreate local patterns of 'what is most at stake for us' in our living and dying. What is most at stake in the context of terminal illness may be different for individuals, yet no matter how contested or fragmented the local world is, there is a shape or coherence which makes them recognisable as a particular form of living and dying. Contemporary Western societies, despite their multicultural complexity, give ideological weight to the ethic of individuality. Yet this individualistic ethic, while proposing the rights of each individual, also creates an emotional and moral weight of uncertainty.

The culture of the local world of terminal illness and care is informed by broader sociocultural beliefs and trends, and is subject to change in ways that emphasise our shared fragility. Not only do terminally ill people and their families face uncertainty, as I discussed in Chapter 5, but health professionals who care for dying people also articulate concerns with the clinical, social, existential and moral uncertainties that are common in the context of contemporary terminal illness and care. These shared uncertainties become part of the cultural climate of terminal care and continually shape the practice of health professionals and the experience of terminally ill patients. The culture of terminal care is informed by biomedical, organisational and moral components which are interdependent. As Good (1994, p. 70) suggests, 'however materialist and grounded in the natural sciences, medicine as a form of activity joins the material to the moral domain'. The 'experts', who include doctors, ethicists, politicians and clergy, cannot provide adequate answers, failing to reach agreement on technical and moral questions relating to the length and quality of life. Medicine has mostly responded by postponing death, rather than simply easing the pain of the final departure. Yet medicine, while framed within a scientific rationalist discourse, is contradictory and haphazard rather than neatly reductive and reflective of an idealised biomedical model. This often appears to be the case in terminal care, where the human elements of suffering and existential crisis cast uncertainties upon the interactions between patients and health professionals.

INDIVIDUALITY AND AUTONOMY

As numerous social scientists including most famously, Marx and his followers have asserted, the advent and take-off of industrial capitalism established a radical individualism in Western societies (Samson 1999, p. 68).

The advent of individualism has had several consequences, including the altering of social relationships in such a way that people are psychologically forced to draw apart from family and friends and to withdraw into the solitude of their own hearts (Tocqueville 1945, p. 104). Perhaps by way of resistance or reaction, greater concern is placed upon the authority of the individual to control the events of life. The concern with patient autonomy is linked to the individualistic focus of contemporary society. A growing dissatisfaction amongst the lay and professional communities with both the power and limitations of medicine further fuels the emphasis that is now placed on autonomy. With regard to the autonomy of dying people, Kellehear (1996, pp. 88–89) has noted that present attitudes towards death are 'forged from the material and social conditions of the baby-boomer generation'. Concern with the individual has become a moral and ethical imperative. Moller (1990) also suggests that the technological development of modern society, with its associated bureaucratic rationality, has created an ideology of individualism. Death is also construed as an individual event, through self-care policies of survival. Individuals are expected to keep their bodies healthy and fit, therefore avoiding illness and death (Elias 1985; Bauman 1992).

The focus upon both the individual and patient autonomy has become a feature of the modern hospice–palliative model of care within contemporary Western societies.

> The principle of autonomy was neglected in terminal care before the development of hospice and palliative care—most patients were ill-informed of their situation, and they were submissive to medical paternalism. The palliative mode emphasised the importance of sensitively informing patients about their state of health and the treatment options available to them, and stressed the importance of patients being involved in decisions about their quality of life (Hunt 1994, p. 131).

Whether the principle of autonomy in terminal care can be traced solely to the development of palliative care is debatable given the social and historical contexts of both individuality in dying and death and the growing consumer dissatisfaction with all medical care. However, palliative care undoubtedly both grew out of, and further fuelled, the impetus for patient autonomy in terminal care, which has now begun to reach beyond the bounds of specialist palliative care. Most recently, patient autonomy in terminal care includes notions of health promotion whereby patients are enabled or empowered to be involved in decision-making (Russell & Sander 1998; Kellehear 1999). The wishes of the individual patient seem to be of prime importance to many palliative care practitioners, as Helen's words reflect:

> If I were to define palliative care I'd say it's about identifying what the patient is wanting. We want them to have some control. Do they want to stay in hospital? If this is the case we are not to say this is wrong.

Some palliative care practitioners also believe that palliative care may not be suitable for every patient, as Jeffrey, a palliative care medical specialist, argues:

> I do not think the fact someone is dying means that some well-intentioned professionals can go in and say this is what we are going to do for you. You have to be invited in . . . you have to allow it to happen the patient's way . . . it may not be the ideal care for everyone . . . if they want to suffer in silence, that's what we have to put up with.

Sam, a palliative care specialist, makes a point of saying to all of his terminally ill patients: 'What is the one thing that you really want? Can we help you achieve this?' However, patients do not often expressly articulate their wishes. Many are too weak to have expectations of achieving much in the last days of their lives. Even if the patients are strong enough, we have to question how able they are to make significant requests when they are infirm in bed and the doctors and nurses are busily going about the routine procedures of their jobs. The issue of power relationships has been the subject of much discussion in the health social sciences (Petersen 1994), but it is particularly significant when the patient in the relationship is often depleted of the physical strength to make his or her wishes known. Some palliative care practitioners are particularly able to put aside the inequalities that exist between practitioner and patient and approach the patient as a person; however, certain practitioners are better able than others to translate this ethic into daily practice.

Not all patients are sweetly compliant —many are cantankerous and demanding. I once observed two nurses caring for Mabel, a patient, who issued a series of instructions relating to her daily care and clinical management for the morning. Mabel wanted her catheter taken out and she insisted on sitting so that when the doctor arrived she could address him properly. Angie, one of the nurses, appeared to resent Mabel's manner and snapped: 'What difference does it make if you are in the bed or the chair?', but Jo, the other nurse, interpreted Mabel's requests differently. She later confirmed with me that she had sensed Mabel's need to have a position which gave an impression of authority. She organised Mabel in her chair and rang to insist that the doctor come to see Mabel straight away to speak to her and to confirm that the catheter could be taken out.

PROFESSIONAL CONTROL AND THE PAIN OF THE DYING PATIENT

Medical dominance and the professionalisation of medical practice are common to the health care systems in Western societies (Friedson 1970a, 1970b; Gordon 1988; Willis 1983). However, I am not as interested here in the macro-context of medicine's state licensed monopoly to practise its art (Daniel 1998, p. 209) as I am in the local worlds of daily interaction between health professionals and patients (Kleinman 1992). Many health professionals do try to understand the suffering of their patients, and realise that a large part of their role as healers is to acknowledge the patients' wishes to have not only security, but also a sense of control. There have been significant changes in the health professional response to dying people in recent years, and much of this can be attributed to the palliative model of care. Yet it would be premature to propose that the authority of the individual dying person has supplanted the biomedical culture and social organisation of medicine. Medicine continues to frame the experience of individuals throughout their illness and dying trajectories. This powerful presence seems a little ironic, given that medicine—with all of its technological mastery—has not wrought much change on the incidence or cure rates of chronic illnesses like cancer (Costain Schou 1993, p. 239). Many health professionals believe that medicine has not reached its potential for easing the burdens of dying people. Implicit in this view is the fundamental belief that, if medicine cannot control death, then at the very least it should control the circumstances of death.

Even within palliative care, where practitioners propose that death is a 'natural' part of life to be accepted when it comes, there is a prominent view that the symptoms of dying should be controlled at all costs. This belief may be rooted, to some extent, in the concept of 'total pain'. Proposed by Cicely Saunders, the concept suggests a paradox whereby physical suffering is humanised, yet the act of 'unlocking' pain encourages the use of power associated with the knowledge and technologies of care (Clark 1999a). An unrelenting approach to the control of symptoms is most often motivated by good intentions, but if it comes at the expense of patient autonomy, it is itself symptomatic of unhealthy medical practice. I accompanied Tony, a palliative care doctor, on a number of 'ward rounds' where I heard him explain to patients that he believed that there was no pain that could not be adequately controlled by 'state of the art palliative medicine'. This belief led him to experiment with various kinds of drugs in order to relieve the pain of terminally ill patients. The 'trial and error' practice of using different drugs in varying combinations is not uncommon in palliative care, and many doctors and nurses quite openly acknowledge the lack of 'scientific rigour' in their practice. The difficulties of treating people with complex physical, social and spiritual problems, as well as the ethical and methodological difficulties involved in implementing experimental drug research in the area, severely restricts research opportunities. Tony treated Gwen, a patient, with a drug he planned to use in a proposed drug trial. Gwen had temporary relief from her pain but was extremely distressed by the side-effects of the medication, which manifested as uncontrollable spasms and shaking. Gwen was simply too frightened and confused to take any control, even if she had been physically able.

Adequate pain control is considered one of the principal tenets of good palliative care. However, there does not seem to be a shared definition of what constitutes 'adequate' pain control. Does 'adequate' mean that pain is controlled to the practitioner's satisfaction or to the patient's satisfaction? Some palliative care practitioners do worry whether total alleviation of pain should be a goal of terminal care, yet many also are caught up with the imperative to treat and to act with the most recent treatments. This view may seem quite understandable when confronted with the physical devastation of diseases like terminal cancer. However, medical and cultural views of suffering overlap to obscure answers for those who seek a 'correct path' to care for dying people, particularly when that path aims to include the individual and his or her family in the decision-making process. June, an experienced nurse, administrator and educator, gave the following example. She expressed a concern that many of the treatments that are used in the attempt to relieve pain and other symptoms may actually prolong the patient's life as well. Her concern was that the patient's quality of life may be compromised:

> Now you take the classic scenario . . . say it's dexamethasone [a drug used for treating swelling particularly in the case of cerebral metastases]. We know it's a hard decision to say cut the dex, because if we cut the dex we know that this particular patient is just going to go down hill very quickly . . . just because the symptoms are controlled doesn't mean they are having quality of life at all. The nurse knows it, the chaplain knows it, the social worker knows it, the cleaner knows it, the cook, everybody knows it and the family are giving very powerful messages to the nursing team—when is it going to be over for him . . . now again that sounds pretty harsh but it's true and then the doctor will say: 'I'm in charge and I say we continue the dex.' Medicine is obviously driving the program—not the needs of the patient or the needs of the family.

Many palliative care practitioners will allow patients to take some control in decisions made about their medical management, although this varies across and within organisations and often depends on the inclinations of individual practitioners. The home care hospice practitioners I have worked with generally express a greater willingness to allow patients to participate in decisions about medical management than do staff that I have observed in inpatient units. The latter group appears to be more concerned with protocols and procedures—and indeed, the regulations of institutions insist that certain rules are kept. Hospice home care practitioners are more willing to admit their limitations, realising that the patients have more power to make their own decisions if they are in their own homes. In one home care team, the staff reviewed the death of Harry, a patient who had obviously been well liked by the team. Marjorie, a palliative care doctor, said: 'He wasn't non-compliant, he just didn't do what we told him to do. He broke up his MS Contin tablets and said that they worked better that way for him. It was fine by me. [MS Contin is a morphine tablet made with a special coating which allows the medication to be released slowly over an extended period of time].' Often, when I visited patients' homes with nurses, the nurse would fill the patient's 'dosett' box (a special box designed to hold tablets for a certain number of days), with various medications, knowing full well that certain patients, particularly some of the older ones, may take some tablets and not others, or might possibly ignore the routine altogether.

THE 'MYTH' OF CONTROL

When I interviewed Maxine, an experienced palliative care nurse, she made the following comments about allowing the patient and the family to have control:

> We burble on about control—you know, palliative care is all about handing control of this person's life back to the patient and back to the family; we don't own the patient and we don't control them. Woe and betide the patient who doesn't do what we want them to do. And they sense this, they will say: 'Well where is this control?' This family that would just give their eye teeth for the morphine to be put up, they will say: 'Well who is really listening to us?' So I think we are really paying a lot of lip service to this issue of control. I think it's mythology, the way the program is going now.

Maxine was not the only practitioner who I interviewed or worked with who expressed this concern, though most often these opinions were expressed by nurses and not doctors. Barbara, an experienced clinical nurse consultant, explained how she had decided to include the patient in the nursing handover discussion, provided that the patient was well enough and agreed to participate. She explained that most of the nurses found the process very difficult because: 'They were so used to talking about the patient to one another, rather than with the patient. Most of them just didn't trust that the patient would understand.' Barbara explained that she wanted to include the patient's experiences in the picture and to try to understand what it was that the patient wanted. When Barbara was present to monitor the handovers, the nurses included the patient. However, when she was not present to oversee the nurses, the process broke down.

There are other instances where patient autonomy and control are clearly constrained by other factors. Patients who ask for euthanasia in the palliative care context are told that this is not possible. They do not have control but are constrained by the moral culture of the palliative care service and by the legal requirements of the state. There is very little empirical evidence to support the level of patient requests for euthanasia in palliative care services, although Hunt and his colleagues (1995) have documented requests in their South Australian service, reporting that 5–10 per cent of patients request a quicker terminal course.

However, many practitioners have told me that it is rare for patients to repeatedly request euthanasia. Bob, a palliative care doctor, said: 'I've been in this game for over ten years and I can count on my one hand the number of times I've been asked.' During the course of my research, the Northern Territory of Australia passed legislation allowing euthanasia, subsequently overturned by the federal government in the Senate (Rose 1997; Quirk 1998). Public debate about euthanasia increased and, according to Tony, a well-known palliative care specialist, this 'lifted the lid off the euthanasia thing'. He reported that he was asked by patients to help them to die an average of about five times a week. Patrick confirmed this, though his estimates were more conservative. Patrick said he had been asked by patients for assistance in dying three times during a period of two weeks at the hospice.

Within the palliative care culture, it appears that the autonomy of the patient is part of a rhetoric that is not always realised. Hunt (1994), who has commented on this aspect of palliative care in Australia, calls this the 'rhetoric–reality gap'. He sees that the unwillingness of Australian palliative care communities to engage in the euthanasia debate reflects their refusal to acknowledge the patient's supreme right to make decisions about the course of the terminal illness and death. In this context, the individual is accepted as an autonomous actor only within the confines of his or her specific culture and time. Foucault (1970, 1972) has argued that interpretations of the individual or self are created through discourses. These discourses profoundly affect what it means to be human and the possibilities for actual individual expression (Petersen 1994, p. 6). Following Foucault, discourses that promote individualism and autonomy in dying may mask certain aspects of choice. These discourses may, in effect, encourage the terminally ill person to make available his or her own subjectivity for management and control. The health professional has certain ways of responding to patient requests, which are drawn from techniques developed theoretically and professionally. These techniques are formulated within the context of biomedical, organisational and moral components of the palliative care culture. However, the health professionals' responses also reflect their own personal values. All of these issues combine with the patients' physical symptoms and emotional distress to create a complex context of ethical decision-making at the end of life, as the following story illustrates.

MARNIE'S STORY

Marnie's story is a fairly dramatic example of what may happen when someone dies. However, it is not entirely atypical of what may happen to terminally ill people during the course of their dying trajectory and it serves as an appropriate example because it combines elements of experiences which are encountered by many patients, families and professional carers. Marnie was a 63-year-old woman with lung cancer and widespread metastatic disease (secondary cancers). She had many problems prior to admission to the inpatient hospice, including: restlessness over weeks, or possibly months, which had been treated with up to six Serepax (a tranquilliser) a day; confusion and agitation; nausea; and feelings of despair which prompted her to ask repeatedly for complete sedation (a continuous infusion of sedative drugs to cause and maintain unconsciousness). Marnie often expressed a wish for 'all this to be over'. The principal reasons for her admission to the inpatient hospice were for symptom control and to relieve her carer daughter, who was very tired. Once Marnie was admitted to the inpatient hospice, some of the staff believed she would spend her last days there, but others disagreed, believing she was capable of returning home to 'live' with her daughter.

It was very clear what Marnie wanted—she wanted to die, and failing this she wanted to be sedated. However, her family were mixed in their responses to her situation. Marnie had been divorced from her husband for fourteen years. Her daughter was exhausted and too distraught to express any consistent opinion, at times asking for her mother to be 'zonked out' and at other times becoming distressed at their inability to communicate with each other. Marnie's son, a nurse, was angry that more was not being done to control her symptoms and distress. The staff in the inpatient hospice had mixed opinions also. Many of the nurses wanted Marnie to be sedated until she died, although the resident doctors believed that her physical strength meant that this could have meant weeks of sedation and could possibly hasten her death. The nurses complained that the doctors were not doing enough for her. Beth said: 'It's like she's in the too hard basket for the doctors.' However, the two resident doctors, Rob and Matthew, felt that with appropriate medications and counselling, Marnie may have some quality life left. Rob explained that she was only 'two months into the diagnosis' and had 'some insight into her condition'. The situation had become quite a 'problem' by the time the clinical team meeting was conducted and the 'case' was discussed at length.

The principal problem seemed to be that no one was entirely sure of what was causing Marnie's symptoms and despair. Was she experiencing severe existential distress? Some of the staff had discovered that she was a 'lapsed' Catholic worrying over what lay in store for her; other staff had sensed unresolved issues with her family. Was her condition related to her medication? Sam, the palliative care specialist, had taken Marnie off the Serepax when she was admitted to the hospice and Matthew thought she may be experiencing withdrawal symptoms. Her doses of morphine at the time of her admission were not entirely controlled and could have influenced her confusion and agitation at that time. Was her condition caused by organic brain syndrome brought on by metastases in the brain? Matthew and Rob were not entirely convinced of this, and they claimed that Marnie often had long periods of lucidity and relative calm. The staff discussed the ethical implications of sedation and whether this was appropriate for Marnie. I noted that the staff took one of two opposing positions about the sedation issue. The two resident doctors, who were specifically responsible for the day-to-day medical management of Marnie, were strongly opposed to sedating her at that particular time. In contrast, the majority of nurses believed that she should be sedated, although Andrew said that he felt uncomfortable with sedating her before she was 'healed'. Eventually it was agreed that, before she was sedated, Marnie should receive some kind of psychological or spiritual support. Everyone agreed that Guy, a psychiatrist experienced in palliative care, should be called in to assess her and that Mary, a Catholic counsellor, should see what she could do to help.

What ensued was distressing for everyone. Marnie was assessed, counselling was attempted without success, and she proved particularly difficult to sedate. I sat with her on one occasion and I understood how distressing her condition was for others to observe. I felt uncomfortable watching her, especially as I knew there was nothing I could do to help her. She had physically pushed over a nurse, thrown a container of water at the chaplain, and would frequently struggle to get out of bed, falling over on at least two occasions. The nurses reported that when they tried to move her she groaned as if she was in pain. I heard her babble unintelligible speech, occasionally calling out 'Help me, oh help me'. She uttered prayers of various kinds. The staff became particularly worried that she might hurt herself or someone else. Marnie needed constant supervision at this stage of her illness. Mary, the Catholic counsellor, was unable to help her in any observable way, although Marnie readily engaged in chanting the prayers that Mary offered in her vigil over the bedside. Marnie was eventually sedated with what the doctors believed were embarrassingly large doses of sedative drugs. She no longer called out or struggled to rise from her bed. Five days later, she developed a chest infection which was not treated, and not long after she died.

While she was still alive, Guy, the psychiatrist, visited Marnie and reported that her symptoms were caused by organic brain syndrome (delirium). However, while the symptoms indicated this condition, the cause of the delirium was not clear. He noted that there was some concern that Marnie may have had an iatrogenic induced acute organic brain syndrome (brought about by the treatments), but that it was impossible to know if this was the case. He suggested that if Marnie were to remain unsedated she would need to be transferred to a psychiatric hospital in order to protect herself and others. Furthermore, if she were transferred to a large public hospital she would automatically be sedated. I noted a marked contrast in the tone of the hospice from the period before and during the unsatisfactory incremental sedation to the period of complete sedation and eventual death. At first the staff could talk of nothing else—Rob lost sleep, Beth cried in frustration and sorrow, and Felicity and Sam spent the morning of ward rounds in the public hospital discussing Marnie in between visiting the patients. When Marnie was completely sedated, she was socially dead. No one spoke about her, though her physical management continued and work around the hospice was 'business as usual'. Sweeting and Gilhooly (1997, p. 93) note that there are degrees of social death whereby 'perceiving a sufferer in ways which could be characterised as socially dead was not necessarily combined with behaving as though they were'. However, in Marnie's case, the behaviours of the staff appeared to match their perceptions of her status as a person.

BIOMEDICAL, MORAL AND ORGANISATIONAL COMPONENTS OF TERMINAL CARE

Marnie's story illustrates how the individual can be lost within her own world of suffering which others cannot know and possibly cannot ever understand. Yet the social network of people surrounding this person must somehow determine what they believe is best for the person and for themselves. How are decisions made? What rules or procedures can help guide the hospice staff and the terminally ill person's family? What can and cannot be done and for what reasons? Marnie asked for sedation, and while this eventually happened, a period of time elapsed where the staff attempted to 'heal' her unsuccessfully. What part did Marnie's choice play in what happened? Clearly, the story that unfolded did not centre on her autonomous decision. Other aspects of the biomedical, organisational and moral components of the palliative care culture impacted upon her experience. Marnie's treatment was justified through technical language and supported by the credibility of an expert. Guy, the psychiatrist, was called to act as an 'independent arbitrator' who could supposedly survey the situation in an objective sense. However, it is notable that Guy's position was legitimated because of his professional position through which he laid claim to a body of rational scientific knowledge. In this context, the knowledge/power nexus is embedded within medical discourse, and by employing the 'clinical gaze' (Foucault 1973; Petersen 1994) Guy and the other doctors were able to lay claim legitimately to a form of social control. The knowledge that doctors claim is especially powerful because it conforms to the 'technical rationality' or 'instrumental reason' associated with Western, science-oriented societies (Petersen 1994, p. 94).

Kleinman (1995, p. 35) discusses how biomedicine's imagery is one of efficacy, where all pathology is 'natural', yet interventions are decidedly 'unnatural':

The burden on the practitioner of the idea of progress is considerable, not least of all through the astonishing claim that ultimately death itself can be 'treated', or at least 'medically managed'. Another aspect of this ideological influence is the euphemization of suffering, which becomes medicalized as a psychiatric condition, thereby transforming an inherently moral category into a technical one.

In Marnie's case, her extreme existential distress was so apparent that it was impossible to ignore, and no doubt the hospice staff were motivated to act for her own good. However, their motives were more complex. It appeared that they also wished to relieve their own discomfort and sense of failure. The decisions they made cannot be judged; however, they can be questioned. The drug administered to Marnie provided an 'institutionally efficient technical fix' (Kleinman 1995, p. 36). While it relieved her apparent suffering, it also relieved the staff of the responsibility of engaging in humanly significant relationships whereby they stood witness to and affirmed the suffering of the individual and the family. Here the biomedical and the moral cultures overlap.

Perhaps Marnie was beyond help due to the advanced state of her disease, but it was interesting to note the easy dismissal of any iatrogenic contribution to her embodied state. The psychiatrist claimed the staff could not know this, therefore responsibility for actions and inactions could not be delegated to any one person or group of people. The hospice staff were prepared to discuss the ethical issues involved in Marnie's story, but there was an unacknowledged air of unease during the meeting. Michael, one of the nurses, said: 'We've been through this before. Remember last year when we had to sedate that noisy man; I felt awful, but it has to be done.' Rob spoke to me the morning after the team meeting and confessed his awful sense of guilt and resentment that he had been forced into making the decision to sedate Marnie. The staff's unease can, in some senses, be linked to the organisational culture of the inpatient hospice. Although it was not stated explicitly during the meeting, I heard from several of the nurses and doctors, in private discussions, that Marnie had to be sedated to protect the staff and the other patients in the hospice. When Michael asked: 'How on earth am I supposed to document all this in the notes?' he received a ready answer from Sam: 'Just record the facts—she is a danger to herself, she lacks dignity and we considered the ethical implications.' Marnie's behaviour was considered dangerous, but it was also disruptive and costly to the hospice as the staff had to supervise her on a 24-hour basis.

SEDATION AND CONTROL

The decisions that were made about Marnie's sedation were influenced by a number of personal and institutional elements which, in turn, were framed by the broader contexts of the biomedical, moral and organisational components of the palliative care culture. Foremost in the minds of Rob and Matthew was the question: 'Will sedation hasten death?' According to Matthew, Sam had said that, in Marnie's case, this may very well happen, but that it could not be helped. This logic offended Matthew and Sam who, fresh from hospital residency after six years of medical school, believed it was their job to 'keep people alive and well'. Felicity counselled them that this was a 'question with no real answer'. She reasoned with the younger doctors: 'My only way of dealing with this is to ask myself—if this were my mother, what would I do? If this were me what would I do?' While these are distinctly moral questions, Matthew, Sam and Felicity were all drawing upon their cultural training for medicine which is, even within the present context, driven by a technological imperative to treat and to cure, and a professional ethic of control. However, Matthew, Rob and Felicity's dilemmas were also informed by their personal thoughts about the value of life and death. Ultimately they expressed their discomfort with having to make judgments about Marnie's treatment.

The manner in which the doctors chose the appropriate medications and dosages for the sedation was also strongly influenced by personal preferences and power plays indicative of the biomedical, moral and organisational components of the palliative care culture. As Atkinson (1995, p. 117) notes, clinical decision-making revolves around an array of practical and theoretical certainties and uncertainties which are rooted in both personal experience and textbook knowledge. However, the actual application of clinical decisions is further complicated by issues to do with hierarchies evident in medical institutions, such as the doctor–nurse power play interaction (Wicks 1995). Angela, the clinical nurse, was angry at Sam's choice of medication because she believed her knowledge in these situations to be superior to that of the specialist, and Felicity drew heavily upon the experience and advice of various specialists who she consulted for advice. Other doctors and nurses questioned Sam's motives for taking Marnie off all of her medication when she entered the hospice. Some suspected that Sam had clashed with the hospice home care doctor who had been responsible for Marnie's management before her admission to the hospice.

I found it particularly interesting that Marnie's sedation should cause such a disruption to the normal routine of the hospice where a large number of the patients are routinely sedated. The disruption occurred partially because there were dissenters in the ranks of the community.

Rob and Matthew were not prepared to accept that Marnie was ready for sedation. They both thought that her sheer physical strength meant she was capable of living longer. In a private discussion with me, Matthew expressed his discomfort. He knew that it was inappropriate to articulate this concern in a more public forum as there was, at that time, a great deal of sensitivity to the issue of sedation in palliative care. Matthew told me that, in his mind, there was no question that sedation and euthanasia were one and the same. Yet expressing this opinion was likely to draw angry responses from many of the practitioners who had been called to justify their practices more openly since the 'euthanasia debate' had begun to gain momentum in the Australian media and in public discourse. This 'sensitivity' to the discussions about euthanasia adds further background to how the story of Marnie unfolded. The hospice staff appeared to pay particular concern to this 'case', whereas in other 'cases' the sedation was not questioned. Australian palliative care services have made a public stand against legalised euthanasia and an Australian Hospice and Palliative Care Association representative presented a report which informed the Senate decision to overturn the Northern Territory of Australia's euthanasia legislation.

Terminal sedation is a common practice in palliative care services, either at the request of the dying person or at the discretion of the health professionals when the dying person is incapacitated. There is no clear definition for this term and a recent article used comments from 61 palliative care experts to propose the term should be abandoned and replaced with 'sedation for intractable distress in dying' (Chater et al. 1998). Clearly the term raises levels of discomfort and uncertainty in some practitioners. However, this assistance—which is given over an extended period while the person dies—is not considered euthanasia by most of the health professionals who work in palliative care. The health professionals use an ethical principle called the doctrine of 'double effect' (Mitchell et al. 1996) to justify sedation. The argument proposes that the principle reason for sedation is not to end the life of the terminally ill person, but to relieve their intractable suffering. However, through the use of sedation, the death of the terminally ill person may, in some cases, be hastened. Any hastening of death is considered the secondary and unintended effect. Sedation is not simply provided to the terminally ill person because it is their 'choice'. Those patients who choose euthanasia are told that this is not possible. It is clear that the moral and ethical principles of the social collective—that is, the palliative care community—determine the boundaries of individual authority over dying. Sedation appears to be an issue where aspects of biomedical, organisational and moral cultures intersect. The following quote by an experienced nurse educator, Deborah, illustrates some of the unease that is experienced by those who try to look critically at their own practice:

Is a good death simply a quiet death with no fuss? Sedation is happening more often and I have to ask is this a way to quiet our own sense of failure? Those in palliative care tend to respond pharmacologically instead of finding the time to listen and talk people through their fears. All you hear about nowadays is midazolam [a sedative drug]. I curse the day midazolam was introduced. Some nurse goes off to a conference and hears about it and figures it should be done in their hospice service. They really know nothing about it at all . . . we seem to have co-opted all the things we went away from.

Deborah's comments suggest that the use of sedation in palliative care is not simply an ethical issue, but one which is closely linked to 'fashions' within medical practice and to the maintenance of the organisation, which favours the 'quiet death with no fuss'.

CONCLUSION

The painful process of dying is particularly uncertain for the terminally ill person and their family; however, uncertainties are also evident for the health professionals who offer care to their dying patients. The time before death for terminally ill patients, as I have illustrated, is fraught with biophysical, social, existential and moral issues which, in the context of contemporary social life, are dealt with in an individualised and private manner. Yet, when health professionals are called upon to facilitate a less painful dying, they inevitably resort to the cultural resources of biomedicine and the organisation in which they work. Palliative care services are particularly aware of respecting the autonomy of the individual and have made many changes which allow patients and their families to be involved in end-of-life decisions. Patients, where possible, can choose where they wish to die and they may refuse certain treatments and request others, like alternative therapies. However, the principle of patient autonomy is always tempered by other aspects of the biomedical, organisational and moral culture of the institutions in which people die. Through discussing the case study of Marnie and the inpatient hospice staff, I have attempted to highlight the way in which biomedical and moral uncertainties are understood and acted upon by the health professionals in the hospice. In Marnie's case, she was unable to participate in the decisions made about her, so the decisions made by the palliative care practitioners illustrate the greater levels of responsibility evident in this example. The way that dying people are 'managed' within society has become one of the principal moral issues of the present historical period. The ethical question of how this is best done raises further uncertainties for terminally ill people, their families and their professional carers.

nine

The rewards and costs of caring

Most members of contemporary Western societies come into intimate contact with a terminally ill or dying person no more than a few times in their lives. Many people will be a witness to only one death—their own. Unable to observe the process of dying and death, we may tend to attribute a certain mystique to this phenomenon which Bauman (1992, p. 2) has called the 'unimaginable other'. Perhaps this is why people who work in the 'dying and death industries', like palliative care and the funeral business, are at the same time respected, but also subject to suspicion. Most people know that when they are faced with dying or bereavement they will want compassionate and professional carers, but they might still be perplexed by the motivations of people who work in the dying and death industries. This chapter analyses the experiences of a group of palliative care nurses who I have worked with during my research. Hopefully, the stories told by the nurses, together with my observations, will give the reader some small understanding of what caring for dying people means to the nurses. In witnessing the dying and death of others and staying with them through pain and sorrow, the nurses rehearse their own dying. Daily, they are reminded of the fragility of their own lives. This chapter is dedicated to those tenacious, spirited women and men who care for terminally ill people. Through their own actions and words we learn how, by sharing a common purpose and philosophy, they can survive this role.

Palliative care nurses do not consider themselves 'special people'; they would rather be thought of as ordinary people doing a 'special job'. These so-called 'ordinary' people, however, are subject to an extraordinary stress imposed by their role as professional caregivers of dying people. The rewards and costs of caring for dying people are indeed complex, for they touch upon embarrassing and painful issues. Perhaps we have something to learn from the nurses who confront their own fragility by working in the presence of death. One of the most valuable lessons the nurses have learned is that, while dying is a lonely and alienating experience (Bauman 1992; Elias 1985), dying people can draw upon the strength and compassion of caring professionals. By banding together to ease the burdens of dying people and their loved ones, palliative care nurses demystify dying and death. Their ethic that death is a natural part of life is not, in this case, a cliché, but serves as a core symbol in a carefully constructed and well-nurtured system of values.

WITNESSING DEATH

It is 2.25 a.m. and the mid-point of night shift at the hospice. This is the first chance since the nurses' handover at nine that Pam has had to sit down and have a cup of tea. She is worried about Barry, a patient who has possibly broken his hip through falling out of bed earlier in the evening. Barry will most probably have to be transferred to hospital in the morning and, as he is in the 'terminal phase', as the nurses call it, he and his family will suffer additionally from this complication. Another nurse, Mary, comments that June, Barry's wife, will be distraught as this is the first night in two weeks that they have been able to convince her to leave Barry's side and go home. She has been sleeping on a makeshift bed in his room at the hospice. June, they agree, is 'the problem' as Barry is 'too far gone to notice'. I sit, watching and listening, caught up in other people's dramas, perhaps their greatest life tragedies: their dying and their grief.

Julie, a nurse I had first met earlier in the evening, rushes into the nurses' staff room where Pam, Mary and I are deep in conversation about Barry. Pale and shaking, she tells us that Mr Garvey, a patient admitted to the hospice only that morning, has just died as she helped him from his bed to go to the toilet. This 'sudden death' has shaken her and she looks visibly upset as she explains that neither she nor Mr Garvey were prepared for the way it happened. Pam takes charge and decides that we will all go to 'assess the situation'. Clustering together, we walk through the darkened hospice, where the patients lie trying to sleep. Often the patients do not sleep because many, the nurses say, are afraid that if they do fall asleep it will be forever. This is my first experience of night shift in a hospice and I think I too would be afraid to sleep, yet many nurses tell me they get so tired they would happily curl up in a spare bed if they could find one.

It takes all three nurses and the stray anthropologist (me) to lift Mr Garvey from the floor to the bed. Pam's comment that he is a 'dead weight' is received with resigned but embarrassed smiles. The nurses are conscious that I am present and I sense that they are not sure whether I will understand. All the same, they try to put the awkwardness aside and piece together Mr Garvey's 'story'. Even though none of the nurses present knew him personally, they try to explain his circumstances from what they have learned from the other nurses. How can it be that a 54-year-old man dies like this—confused and in pain, with apparently no close family or friends and with little understanding of the progression of his disease and the nearness of his death? Julie leaves and Pam and Mary begin to prepare the body. To my inexperienced eye, Mr Garvey does not look as bad as many of the other patients I have seen here. At first I was shocked at the sight of their darkly bruised and weeping skin, their open wounds smelling of decay, their catheters attached to bags full of blood and urine and their wasted bodies that are propped up by numerous pillows and caged in standard hospital beds. Then Pam and Mary undress Mr Garvey and I see his sunken chest and puny arms hanging from his bony shoulders. His cancerous body lies naked and vulnerable, sexless and lifeless. The nurses, however, continue to treat Mr Garvey as they would have just fifteen minutes before and they take care in their washing, drying and powdering. Mr Garvey does not have any talcum powder and Pam borrows some Johnson's Baby Powder from the next patient who shares a bathroom with this room. They say they will shave him but cannot find a razor or shaving cream. Mary packs Mr Garvey's anus with a cotton swab to prevent leakage, as he will remain in the hospice for the night before the funeral directors come to take him away. And then they hunt through a hastily packed bag and find only a crumpled T-shirt and a pair of faded baggy shorts. I help to dress Mr Garvey in this pathetically incongruous outfit and Mary tenderly combs his unkempt and surprisingly full head of hair. We lay him out carefully, propping his chin up with a folded towel and crossing his arms over his chest, trying as best we can to shape his sorry body into the semblance of a dignified corpse. We look down at him in embarrassed silence. This is the best we can do.

When I speak to Mary later, she says: 'I hate it when it's like that. He's had no time here, he had no one to help him through it. I don't feel as if I've really done my job.' Mary expresses what so many nurses feel in these kinds of situation. They want to make a difference, a commitment to making it as good as it can be, but they also sense that somehow much of this is really beyond their control.

SHARED VALUES IN THE FACE OF DEATH

One of my central arguments throughout this book is that death overshadows our lives, reminding us all of the fragile nature of life itself. However, as humans we are made stronger through cultural and social life and our greatest challenges to the threat of death are most successfully instituted as a social group. The nurses depicted in this chapter build a system of values which provides a focus for their work and ultimately gives meaning to their lives. This sentiment is most eloquently reflected in the words of Saunders & Baines (1983, pp. 65–66), who base their comments on many years of monitored practice and research at St Christopher's Hospice, which is considered the founding organisation within the hospice movement:

> The resilience of those who choose and continue to work exclusively in this field is won by a full understanding of what is happening and not by a retreat behind a technique . . . if we are to remain for long near the suffering of dependence and parting we need also to develop a basic philosophy and search, often painfully, for meaning even in the most adverse situations.

These sentiments illustrate that values 'regulate the effects of experience by regulating the meaning and importance of the experience' (Pearlin 1989, p. 249). Until recently, the influence of 'social values' on the experience of stress has not been adequately dealt with in sociological literature; however, it has been noted that anthropologists have paid particular attention to the 'cultural context', of stressors (Jacobson 1989, p. 257). Stressors, within the 'cultural context', are viewed as threats to a shared system of values.

The shared system of values is defined by what a group of people consider to be of importance. These shared values are closely related to collective goals and to personal and group feelings of efficacy. Palliative care nurses develop and share a system of values that is built upon the 'hospice philosophy'. Aiming to provide person-centred 'holistic' care, palliative care teams care for the dying person's physical, psychological, social and spiritual needs. Often stress is related not just to a personalised affront to individual values, but a threat to the shared meanings of the group. If the nurses are misunderstood or looked upon with suspicion, their reason for being and for providing care to dying people is undermined. The strategies that nurses employ to cope with the stress display a negotiated logic. Perceptions of stress and strategies for coping, therefore, are not entirely idiosyncratic, but are grounded in a learned logic that is systematically shared. This contextual approach does not exclude the structural components of stress, particularly those that relate to status and roles within social institutions (Pearlin 1989), but incorporates elements of structurally determined stress into a broader sociological framework. Stress, in this context, is not associated with psychological disorder, nor with matters of structure 'superimposed upon such disease-oriented models'; it 'is not an inherent attribute of external conditions, but emanates from discrepancies between those conditions and characteristics of the individual—his or her needs, values, perceptions, resources, and skills' (Aneshensel 1992, p. 16). Even though the experience of stress is individually felt, perceptions of what is stressful and responses to stress are learned and shared within social networks.

Perhaps to the uninitiated observer, the most obvious source of stress for the nurses would be to witness terrible grief, as Paul's comment illustrates: 'Of course it's sad, sometimes you lose the plot a bit, you just have to deal with it.' However, the nurses' stress is far more complex and is embedded within a contextual web of experience. As Hinds and her colleagues (1992) have noted, the context should be seen as interactive layers of experience which take into account both individual and imme-diate experiences, as well as the more general organisational and cultural milieu. The stress associated with nursing dying people and caring for patients' families is both socially and personally constructed. The nurses' sources of stress exist in several different contexts. They are found within the nurses' own existential struggles with the meaning of death and within the exchanges they have with the people around them. However, sources of stress are also found within the images presented in the media and in the subtle signs of non-verbal communication which abound in the world around them. Despite the numerous idiosyncratic episodes of stress, there is a unifying principle within the contextualised layers of experience. This means that we understand stress because together we construct meanings that are associated with different kinds of experiences.

THE STRESS OF NURSING THE DYING

Facing death, whether it be our own, that of someone we love dearly, or someone we feel responsible for, presents us with a unique challenge. For most of us, this happens infrequently; however, this is not the case for palliative care nurses, who may witness one or more deaths every single working day. Inevitably these frequent contacts with dying people awaken some personal response (Stedeford 1984). According to Carol, a very compassionate nurse: 'We cry with the best of them . . . if you've given a bit of yourself to them, you lose that something when they die.' However, constantly dealing with death is not only sad, it is confronting: 'If you work here you have to be aware of your own mortality, you've got to have a certain presence of mind,' Paul said. Most of the nurses I worked with agreed that personally facing death was an issue that could not be ignored, but it was also one that brought a surprising level of reassurance to them, as Jacqui said: 'I've learnt that death can indeed be peaceful as opposed to violent.' As can be seen from these examples, familiarity with death evokes both comfort and grief. And while these conflicting emotions and beliefs are often shared, sometimes the nurses themselves question the value system they have put in place to give meaning to their work. This form of doubt acts as a threat to their shared value system and may precipitate a form of 'collective' stress as much as a personal response, as evidenced in the following example.

One of the palliative care services I observed has a 'separation review' incorporated into its weekly team clinical meeting. It is a formal means, once the patient has died, of discussing the circumstances of the illness, death and associated care. This form of self-evaluation requires the doctors and nurses to make a judgment as to the 'outcomes' of the service. They ask: 'Was the outcome satisfactory to the patient, the family, and the team?' At one meeting, Tania decided to challenge the validity of the evaluation, suggesting that the question relating to the patient was 'silly'. 'After all,' she said, 'none of them wants to die . . . who wants to die? . . . How can a patient be satisfied with us helping them to die?' This comment was followed by an embarrassed silence, with the question of 'Who wants to die?' left unanswered.

It has been widely documented in sociological and associated litera- ture that both support and stressors often reside in the same sets of interactions (Lynam 1990; Tilden & Gaylen 1987; Atkinson et al. 1986; Hammer 1983). The personal networks developed by the palliative care nurses between family, friends and colleagues feature as a source of both stress and support. It is not unusual for the nurses to report that 'It's hard to talk about it at home' or, as Maureen said: 'My husband doesn't find it easy to talk about it [death], he'll listen but he won't ask, so I don't bring my work home.' Anne explained her feelings in this way:

> You know it's not arrogance that we don't confide in our families. What we do is special and only we can understand really what it's like. We don't want to burden them with something they don't need to know. When I first started here I'd go home and tell the kids about it, thinking this is good for them, you know—educational, but then I thought this is really not fair and now I just leave them be.

Nurses tend to turn to their fellow workers for support when they feel overly burdened in their care of the dying because there is more chance that their colleagues will understand. This is particularly evident in palliative care nurses rather than in nurses who work, for example, in oncology units (Plante & Bouchard 1996). However, some palliative care nurses, like Emily and Joanne, felt strongly that there was a 'level of dishonesty' and a 'conspiracy of silence'—that by admitting to personal pain they were conceding that they could not cope. Many of the more experienced nurses had, however, built up strong social support networks with their colleagues. The ambivalent responses to the question of honesty do, however, indicate an area of implicit and often unrecognised stress. The system of values shared by the nurses and implicit in the hospice philosophy features 'openness', and certainly honesty, yet the appropriateness or the context of honesty itself is, for the nurses, problematic and in many cases stressful.

It is not just the family, friends and colleagues of the palliative care nurses who often don't seem to understand the joys and sorrows of caring for dying people and their loved ones. Elsewhere in this book I have discussed the historical and social contexts of death awareness (Kubler-Ross 1969; Metcalf & Huntington 1991) and death avoidance or acceptance (Elias 1985; Kellehear 1990; Walter 1991). I believe that there have been significant changes in the way people in contemporary Western societies regard dying and death. Dying and death no longer seem taboo and many people are prepared to discuss many aspects of the topic. However, this newfound 'permissiveness regarding death' (Schneidman 1984, p. 4) appears more academic or intellectualised than is immediately apparent in everyday interactions. The nurses agree that dying and death are still subjects that most people would rather not discuss. Mandy reflected this feeling: 'They change the subject, they shuffle their feet.' Margaret used the following words when she spoke with her colleagues at a seminar:

> Let's face it, there's no high profile of death and dying. In our culture most people don't want to talk about death, except of course, for people like us. They think of death as something that only happens to other people.

Many nurses do not speak openly to acquaintances about the nature of their work. 'I tell them I work at Meadowvale, not the hospice' and 'I say I work for the domiciliary nursing service, but I don't mention hospice' are just two of the many comments that were made by nurses. In circumstances outside of the palliative care context, nurses often find it easier to avoid talking about the exact circumstances of their job. Many nurses indicated that they thought people outside of the palliative care 'system' lacked an understanding of what was involved in caring for the dying.

One of the most stressful experiences for the nurses is when they feel they are unable to do their job, when they fail to 'make a difference' for the dying person and their family. If the patient, their family and friends, and the nurse have had a 'good' death experience, the nurse validates her sense of self-worth and the system of values shared by palliative care health professionals. 'Bad' deaths, however, are problematic as well as physically and emotionally exhausting for those who participate

114 FRAGILE LIVES

in the nursing care. At the beginning of this chapter, I told the story of Mr Garvey who died suddenly during the night before the nurses felt they had a chance to get to know him and to help him. The nurses present felt they had failed Mr Garvey, though they were not sure what they could have done to change the situation. Other instances that nurses report as being stressful are when patients die young, do not accept their approaching death, or when they seem to give up completely by refusing to interact with those around them.

A story I was told seems to capture a tragic sense of hopelessness that many nurses sometimes feel and that obviously burdened Jacqui, the nurse who bravely bore witness to the tragedy. Early in her career as a palliative care nurse, Jacqui cared for Jenny, a 23-year-old divorced woman who had a four-year-old child. Jenny had survived a disastrous and violent marriage, but could not overcome cancer of the cervix which had aggressively taken over her body and was then taking away her life. But Jenny, like so many other young cancer sufferers, was angry and denied her imminent death. With few material goods, all she had to organise before her death was a guardian to look after her little girl. Jenny was forced to stay with her estranged parents and she had no contact with the father of her child. Jacqui tried her hardest to encourage Jenny to address the issue of guardianship and to resolve her differences with her family, but Jenny resolutely refused until the weekend of her death. Jenny's parents rushed out to get a will from a newsagency while, in extreme pain and refusing medication, Jenny vomited copious amounts of 'old' blood. Jacqui recalled desperately trying to disguise this distressing episode from Jenny's confused daughter, who looked on. Jenny signed a will; Jacqui gave her some much-needed medication and climbed into bed with her to cradle her in her arms until she died. But, as Jacqui said, there was nothing at all dignified about this death and she privately grieved over it for the following eight years. Jacqui told me that every time she drove anywhere near the location of the death, a knot formed in her stomach and her normally happy outlook changed to overwhelming sorrow.

Many of the difficulties and stresses that palliative care nurses experience in their care of those who are dying relate to the structural conditions of their work (Benoliel 1983; Vachon 1987, 1995; Field 1989; Plante & Bouchard 1996). Often a tension arises between the nurses' goals, which are concomitant with their value system, and the maintenance of the organisation. The demands of their work do not always allow them the kind of time and freedom of involvement which is conducive to building good relationships with their patients, as Suzanne relates:

> One of the most frustrating things is the bell . . . it rings and it's someone looking for the keys to the drug cabinet and you've got to go

and open it up with them—and of course it's just when you are having a nice chat with a patient—they may even be ready to tell you something really important. That really is stressful.

James (1989) conducted a study in a hospice and found, amongst other things, that the demands of physical work interfered with the nurses' commitment to holistic care. The nurses tended to accept a commonsense understanding of 'work' as physically carrying out a certain task. Other work, such as 'emotional labour', was carried out only as 'time' allowed. Plante and Bouchard (1996) found that the short time permitted to accomplish palliative care nursing duties was especially significant.

Other sources of stress for the nurses which potentially threaten their sense of competence and possibly make them feel they have failed are when patients are non-compliant with medications, and various other anomalous experiences which disrupt the routine of the organisation. Sudden and traumatic deaths like those of Mr Garvey and Jenny are a cause of concern for the nurses. A prolonged dying experience can be equally as stressful as Robyn, echoing a sentiment expressed by many nurses, honestly commented: 'Sometimes you think: "For God's sake, die", the family are ready, we [the palliative care organisation] are ready, but the patient won't.' Unexpected and anomalous experiences delay the nurses' strategy of collective forgetting (Glaser & Strauss 1966). It is important to learn to 'forget' tragedy, as Glaser and Strauss note; however, other more recent research (Maeve 1998) suggests that nurses use the dilemmas of the patients' lives to inform their own personal and professional lives through a process of 'weaving a fabric of moral meaning'. The nurses in my study often delayed forgetting by discussing difficult deaths and worrying about their possible failure. However, they also attempted to justify what they were doing or, in Maeve's words, 'weave a fabric of moral meaning' into their lives.

SURVIVING THE CARE: SHARED STRATEGIES AND VALUES

In order to contain the impact of the stress associated with caring for the dying, palliative care nurses employ various coping strategies and engage in reciprocally supportive interactions. While most nurses have a personal repertoire of coping techniques, I am emphasising those techniques which are based upon their shared system of values, a system which gives meaning to their work and ultimately to their lives. Their formal and informal networks of support are focused within the palliative care community, which also consolidates the value system they share. Much of the interaction and language employed within the palliative care community is contextualised in a world where dying and death are familiar. Often the behaviours and comments of the nurses and their other colleagues challenge the conventional understanding of private and highly controlled management of dying and death.

In Chapter 6 I discussed how the medical model is still firmly rooted in the curative process which has construed death as a failure. However, many doctors and nurses no longer see dying and death as a reflection of their failure to sustain life (Wilkes 1986). Field (1989, p. 140) attributes this change largely to the hospice movement, which has been able to demonstrate patient-centred holistic care for dying people. The palliative care nurses I have worked with are unified in their belief that dying and death can be 'good', although, as I have indicated, certain situations are often beyond the control of the group of nurses. The nurses reverse the definition of 'death as failure' to 'death as potentially good'. They also employ the terminology of winning and losing in a similar context of reversal. I heard an example of this kind of logic in the corridor of one of the hospices I visited. A doctor and a group of nurses discussed a patient who had died that morning. The doctor commented on how they had 'won' the 'case', the patient having been both psychologically prepared and medically well controlled. The nurses agreed that the patient could so easily have been 'lost', considering the circumstances of her physical and social situation. The hospice staff 'won' because it was a 'good' death. This form of parlance is common within the palliative care community, but is in direct contrast to popular idiom where people 'give up the fight' or 'lose the battle' with cancer and where doctors and nurses 'lose' their patients.

Sometimes, despite the good intentions of the nurses, the dying and death of a patient may not be good. Nurses cope with the anomalous experiences, such as the patient who tragically remains distressed and will not accept death, by deliberately problematising the situation. Considerable discussion, which may be in formal meetings or corridor and lunch room talk, allows the nurses to shift the responsibility away from themselves to the individual patient or perhaps to the family of the patient, even more broadly to the 'society' which has allowed this social problem to arise. In this way, the nurses accept the patient's autonomy, relinquish control and displace the stress they feel when things do not go according to plan. As Angela, a palliative care administrator, commented: 'We do what we can to fulfil obligations . . . we become involved, but not enmeshed.' Angela also reports that a death that is good is 'when everything goes well', although she says: 'Often things don't go well.' Palliative care nurses commonly pursue both formal and informal reflexive strategies in order to systematically and periodically examine common goals and procedures. Formal evaluations are initiated and organised by administrative personnel, while informal methods of evaluation are conducted on a personal level as well as within groups of varying size. The 'separation review', noted previously, is an example of this kind of meeting. These meetings primarily provide opportunities to discuss clinical management problems, and are promoted by administrative staff as an opportunity to evaluate outcomes and goals. Other meetings include the nursing handover, the weekly clinical meetings, various seminars and training sessions, as well as social and spontaneous gatherings. Both the formal and informal gatherings are not just forums for virtuous self-appraisal; they are used to voice self-doubts and to direct criticisms towards 'competing systems of care'—most commonly those associated with mainstream medicine that emphasise cure at the expense of good palliative care.

Both self-doubts about ability or belief and competing systems of care threaten the value system the nurses use to validate their work. Open discussion in both formal and informal gatherings allows nurses the opportunity to reassure one another and to group together in opposition to what they perceive as threats. This opposition is expressed in stories about the failure of mainstream medicine to deal adequately with the needs of dying people. Seale (1989, p. 552) discusses James' unpublished PhD thesis (1986) on care and work in nursing the dying, noting that nursing staff find justification for their expertise in telling stories amongst themselves about hospitals' failures to cope with terminally ill patients. Wright (1981) also found that hospice staff express similar forms of criticism which they use to justify their own practices. The nurses' reassurances to one another and shared expressions of opposition, therefore, act as ways of justifying both their expertise and their beliefs.

Palliative care service administrations are aware of the need to provide adequate support systems for their staff (Hospice Care Service 1993; Astrom et al. 1993; Athlin et al. 1993). External counselling services are often made available at no cost to the staff. Nurses do, however, actively negotiate their own support systems from within and outside of the palliative care environment. It has been noted previously that nurses most commonly turn to their colleagues for support, while often not confiding in their families. Even though nurses justify this behaviour as not wanting to burden their families, their choice of support system also serves other functions. By choosing not to confide in their families and friends, nurses may first avoid any challenge to their value system, and second create a 'non-hospice' space or a retreat from work. The nurses share a particular world-view with their colleagues. This world-view is one in which dying and death are normalised—it is commonplace and, within the context of the palliative care environment, less frightening and more within their shared control.

Without exception, all of the nurses in this study spoke of the importance of the 'team' in creating a supportive environment. This interdisciplinary and supportive approach has been integral to hospice care since its founding days at St Christopher's Hospice in London. Openness to patients, but also to other staff members, is not just desirable, but is explicitly incorporated into the general ethos of palliative care. There is not simply a desire, but an expectation that nurses will turn to one another for support, as Dave said: 'If you can't turn to your workmates, who can you turn to?' The act of sharing experiences consolidates the networks of support, and works to validate and strengthen the value system of the nurses. June, a retired nurse, made the comment:

> You know we are not so special, we are just ordinary people in a special situation, doing a special job . . . but we are in it together, working for the same things, for people's rights to dignity . . . that's what's so important.

Intimacy is encouraged amongst the nurses and their other colleagues by telling stories and sharing in an established pattern of palliative care humour. Although the levels of intimacy vary within interdisciplinary teams of workers, those teams that appeared closely knit seemed more likely to engage in 'outrageous' humour. All we have to do is think of the number of jokes that incorporate death to understand that humour is widely used to disperse the fear of dying and death. The humour used in hospice and palliative care communities is decidedly 'black' and confined to the context of the immediate environment, though not within the hearing of the patients. It is usually considered appropriate, although some nurses displayed a degree of embarrassment most likely associated with my presence. It might be hard for 'outsiders' to understand how a palliative care team, in the words of a well-respected professor of palliative care, 'fall about in hysterics while being surrounded in tragedy'. However, this is part of the distinctive world-view of palliative care—you have to be part of it to really understand, and this is why the nurses turn first and foremost to their colleagues for support.

CONCLUSION

In this chapter, I have addressed the areas that palliative care nurses perceive as stressful and have conceptualised shared coping strategies and social supports that are negotiated by the nurses in the course of their work. These conceptualisations are reflections of collective, dynamic actions that act to affirm the resourcefulness of the individuals and groups studied, but also highlight the importance of human agency in confronting opposing values and structurally imposed barriers to desired goals. Palliative care nursing is different from many other forms of nursing, as Suzanne reflected:

> We practise good basic nursing care here—treating the person, not the disease. There is no time to do this in ordinary hospitals, there it's as if the person is the disease. Here we let people die . . . we don't feel as if we've failed.

Palliative care nurses find their work personally and professionally satisfying. 'It's not just a job, it's not monetarily driven,' Jacqui said. 'It's a privilege—I feel humbled by visiting a huge range of people, from the poor to the extremely wealthy.' Suzanne spoke about how she had learned so much from the people who had shared their life experiences and their wisdom with her: 'I have changed . . . your priorities change here, I value life more.' The women and men who have tried palliative care nursing and continue in this demanding field share similar goals, ideas and philosophies to those recorded here. Many nurses try this kind of nursing and leave within months; others 'burn out'. But many stay despite the physical, emotional, ethical, social and spiritual problems they encounter through the course of their work.

Many of the stresses encountered by the palliative care nurses relate to the sensitive nature of their work. Not only are their patients frail, ill and frightened, the patient's families and friends are themselves vulnerable, unwillingly thrust into the act of final parting and entering the grieving process even before the death of a loved one. These deaths remind the nurses of their own mortality and the fragile and fleeting nature of life itself. I have deliberately sought to highlight the sociological nature of stress and coping by illustrating how the palliative care nurses' sources of stress, their coping strategies and their choice of support relate to their system of shared values. Corr and Corr (1983, p. xi) make it very clear that 'hospice is a philosophy, not a facility', that recognises that 'dying and mourning are normal parts of life'. Palliative care nurses embrace this philosophy, building a value system that gives meaning to their work and lives and enabling them to cope with the stress of caring for the dying. Their system of shared values is a challenge to death and to the fragile nature of our lives—it reassures the nurses and all they work with, and indeed it reassures all of us that dying is part of life. The challenge the nurses collectively propose reassures all of us that, while we must pass over to death alone, we need not die alone.

ten

Palliation: Masking pain or masking death?

Dying and death have always been diabolically disruptive to individuals and to the societies they live in. Life is always fragile in the face of death but it is interesting to reflect upon the ways that we temper this fragility through our management of dying and death. The hospice movement and, more recently, the development of palliative care and palliative medicine, can be seen as part of a contemporary response to the medical management of dying. Hospice was originally conceived as part of a broader 'death awareness movement' which impacted upon Western advanced industrialised societies in the 1960s and 1970s (Metcalf & Huntington 1991, p. 25). However, I suggest that recent developments within palliative care and palliative medicine now reflect a specialisation in dying and death. This specialisation is framed by medicine and by mainstream health care, a move which has brought both benefits and disadvantages to terminally ill people, their families and those who care for them. This chapter traces some of the changes in the original hospice movement through to the contemporary context of palliative care and palliative medicine. It was unrealistic to expect that the original ideals of the hospice movement would survive intact, but what interests me is how the medical component of palliative care overrides the less scientific or the intuitive aspects of this potentially unique form of care.

As I have indicated in previous chapters, the less scientific or the 'softer' aspects of palliative care focus on accommodating the patient's choice within a flexible institutional structure. Principally, the element of individual choice and, to a lesser degree, the variation in practices and structures are reflections of a broader postmodern condition. 'Postmodern death' typifies a fragmentation of ideas and behaviours, a multivocality of responses and, ultimately, an existential uncertainty. Kastenbaum (1993a, p. 76) notes that 'as society becomes "postmodern" it also becomes vulnerable to the attenuation or loss of beliefs, values, and communication patterns that had provided it with a sense of identity and continuity.' The palliative care philosophy recognises the multiplicity of beliefs and communication patterns evident in the collective of dying patients. Nevertheless, care is organised scientifically by a process which categorises different diseases through comparison and similarity. Using this framework, 'pathological normality' (disease is normalised around signs and symptoms) and routinised pharmacological responses appear to offer more certain answers to the uncertainty of dying than psychological, social and spiritual counselling and support. This chapter considers the argument that palliative care may, by focusing on the medical responses to the pain associated with dying, in some way mask or cover the actual process of dying. This argument is not at all straightforward because the pain associated with dying is complex and medicine is efficient in relieving some of that pain. Nevertheless, rational scientific approaches to pain and dying will not ultimately give meaning to the experience of suffering. The changes that are taking place in the practice of palliative care are therefore reflective of a broader social process which manifests in a tension between postmodern death and the medical management of death. Where postmodern dying finds us bereft of ways to approach death as a collective, medicalised dying pushes the phenomenon of death away through technology and pretence.

THE HOSPICE MOVEMENT AND PALLIATIVE CARE

The modern hospice movement has grown from its origins in 1967 at St Christopher's Hospice in London (Stoddard 1978; du Boulay 1984; Clark 1998) to encompass a method of caring for dying people which is interpreted variously in many parts of the world. Hospice care is now practised in over 60 countries around the world (Kastenbaum 1993b) and since its inception has been promoted as an approach which brings a holistic philosophy to the care of terminally ill people and their families (Corr & Corr 1983; James & Field 1992; Clark & Seymour 1999). As an alternative, hospice, as it has been practised in Western societies, has served as a symbolic critique of how dying people are managed in other medical settings. These mainstream medical settings have been criticised as inappropriate, technologically driven and overly clinical (Muller &

Koenig 1988; Moller 1990; Slomka 1992; Weber 1995). The hospice approach has therefore been praised as a welcome change from the curative model of medicine that views death as a failure (Siebold 1992; Davis & George 1993). Regardless of geographical location or the context of historical development, hospice is generally associated with a social movement. In this sense, it has much in common with other contemporary social movements such as the women's movement and the ecological movement, attracting an international and diverse constituency (Siebold 1992, p. 7). These kinds of movement often take an idealistic or moralistic stance and are, in some contexts, marginal to the mainstream of society (Lofland 1996, p. 2).

In 1990, Maddocks (1990, p. 535), a professor of palliative care, noted that 'hospice', 'terminal care' and 'palliative care' were all used in Australia because the name for the new discipline was then not consistent. He made it clear that 'palliative care' was the favoured term. Terminal care can refer to any manner of care used in the last weeks of a person's life, and may include intensive and surgical procedures (Molloy & Clarnette 1993). 'Hospice' and 'palliative care' are still used interchangeably, though hospice is now less common. Although early discussions stressed that hospice was not a place or a facility but a philosophy (Frey 1981; Corr & Corr 1983; Jacobsen 1985), the term 'hospice' is now used most commonly in relation to an inpatient facility. The term 'palliative' first came to be associated with hospice care in Canada and the United States in 1975 because 'hospice' was thought to connote 'custodial or less than optimal care' (Saunders 1993, p. 79). Doctors also believe 'the term palliation is more palatable to both physicians and patients since it does not imply giving up completely with no hope in sight as does the perception of hospice' (Enck 1993, p. 1). While the terms 'palliative care' and 'hospice' have continued to be used interchangeably in recent medical and nursing literature, the term 'palliative care' predominates, and there is now an increasing distinction drawn between palliative care and palliative medicine. In establishing this distinction, Australia, for example, has implemented a speciality stream of palliative medicine within the College of Physicians (Maddocks 1994). The specialist versus the generalist debate in palliative care and the distinction drawn between palliative care and palliative medicine continues to create interest in many countries around the world, including Canada, Australia and the United Kingdom. Clark & Seymour (1999, p. 79) note that the 'scope for confusion in the usuage and application of these labels is clearly apparent and indicates the value of a close examination of their differences and similarities'.

Palliative care is now practised in two different contexts: first, as a specialty, by the hospice and palliative care services; and second, in a general sense, by health professionals who work in the mainstream health care services. The specialist form of palliative care is provided by multidisciplinary teams of professionals which include doctors and nurses, and may include psychologists, social workers, physiotherapists, occupational therapists, chaplains and other pastoral care workers. The volunteers so essential to the original hospices (Field & Johnson 1993) now play less of a role in Australia, though still contribute support to patients and their families. Palliative care, as it is provided in the mainstream health care services, may be provided by general practitioners, specialist doctors of various disciplines, and hospital and domiciliary nurses. In this context, palliative care may be provided to patients with a range of illnesses of a terminal nature, for varying lengths of time, including those patients who die in acute care or critical care settings (Danis et al. 1999; Hockley 1999; Weissman et al. 1999). Rather than adopting the distinctive philosophy associated with specialist palliative care, this latter form of care focuses more broadly on quality-of-life issues during terminal illness. As Clark and Seymour (1999, p. 86) have observed in the United Kingdom, there is a distinction drawn between the delivery of palliative care and the philosophy of palliative care.

Hospice care has traditionally been associated with cancer, where 'death can be predicted with a reasonable degree of certainty as the disease progresses, even though the timing of death may not be precise' (WA Hospice Palliative Care Association with the Health Department of WA 1995, p. 23). Ideally, however, hospice and palliative care is thought to be appropriate for people who are dying from all kinds of illnesses where they may need long-term care (Field & Addington-Hall 1999). However, as Field and Addington-Hall note, there are substantial barriers to extending specialist services to all people who may need palliative care, including the levels of skill of specialists, the difficulty in determining who should receive palliative care, the attitudes of the recipients of care and the resource implications.

The historical roots of the modern hospice movement have been firmly planted in, and have grown from, spiritual and theological soil (Frey 1981; Corr & Corr 1983; Bradshaw 1996). By contrast, palliative care has a medical basis and is derived from the Latin word *pallium* meaning to cloak, mask or cover, involving the cloaking of symptoms with treatments aimed to comfort the patient (Twycross 1995, p. 2). Palliative care is thought to have arisen as a medical domain alongside the hospice movement (Goodlin 1997, p. 13). Both hospice and palliative care involve dying and death, but where the former has tended to concentrate on facilitating a good death, the latter focuses on the comfort of the patient, principally through symptom relief.

The practice of palliative care focused on comprehensive symptom management for patients who were often being bypassed in busy hospital practice. Although slow to gain recognition by the medical establishment, palliative care has gradually evolved into a specialist discipline (Maddocks 1999, p. 63).

The symptoms associated with dying are complex, but usually include physical symptoms such as pain, nausea, vomiting, constipation, breathlessness and so on, and these are principally treated through medical means. In this chapter I argue that not only has the development of palliative care masked the symptoms associated with dying, it has also masked the original intention of the hospice movement. Many of the more recent organisational developments in palliative care, such as the growth of the professional discipline and the incorporation of palliative care within mainstream medical and nursing practice, indicate a movement to reinstate the medical focus of terminal care within the hospice/palliative care domain. This focus, as I have discussed in Chapter 6, promotes a salvational view of medicine, unlike the original hospice movement which sought to encourage acceptance of death as part of normal living and dying.

SOCIOLOGICAL CRITIQUES

The development of the hospice movement has been subject to sociological analysis in Britain (Seale 1989, 1991; Clark 1991, 1993b, Clark 1998, 1999a, 1999b); James & Field 1992; Bradshaw 1996; Clark & Seymour 1999), the United States (Abel 1986; Mor et al. 1989; Siebold 1992) and in Australia (McNamara et al. 1994). It appears that many of the initial goals set out by pioneers such as Cicely Saunders have been achieved and that dying people do receive better and more compassionate care in many instances. Yet there have also been many problems associated with the rapid expansion of the hospice movement in both Britain and the United States, and many of the initial goals have been compromised. Clark (1993a, p. 7) notes that while the British movement has claimed to offer an alternative view of the dying process 'to that prevailing in modern, bureaucratic societies', hospice faces a number of pressures which threaten to undermine the original goals. Many of these pressures are documented, and range from broad-ranging sociological analysis considering the charismatic birth and subsequent routinisation and bureaucratisation of the social movement (James & Field 1992) to issues of policy and practice and the creeping medicalisation of a community-led movement (Clark 1993b; Corner & Dunlop 1997).

Australian hospice and palliative care has developed differently from the British movement, although Australian developments reflect British concerns. Anthony, a well-known authority in palliative care, suggests that both Australia and the United Kingdom share similar philosophies and practices, both being 'driven by structural determinants, such as the health care organisation'. There seems little doubt that, in both countries, the original 'hospice vision', which proposed the reconstruction of care for terminally ill people and challenged the medical and societal view of dying and death, has changed. Within the palliative context of care many terminally ill individuals and many of the practitioners who contribute to organisational culture carefully manage, and otherwise remain ambivalent about, the issue of death. One example of this ambivalence is in the notable change in communication patterns demonstrated in the work of Field and Copp (1999), who reviewed an array of literature about communication and dying in modern Western societies. They found that there has been a trend away from the open communication established from the 1960s onwards to a 'conditional' form of discussion about death. I believe this 'conditional' approach is used not just in mainstream health care, but also in specialised palliative care services. Dying and death are, in this context, highly individualised, yet also highly managed.

Palliative care has, over the past ten years, become a less well-defined concept. Some fear that it has now become a form of supportive care for people who have progressive diseases of a terminal nature, but of uncertain duration. Biswas (1993, p. 135), a British nurse administrator, draws important distinctions between terminal care and palliative care, which she links to an increasing medicalisation of hospice and palliative care:

> The shift from terminal care to the much wider area of palliative care is a shift in emphasis which alters the original concept of improving care of dying people. Palliative care shifts the focus of attention away from death and there is a real danger that, by talking about and focusing upon palliation, people may stop talking about and confronting the fact that the individual is going to die.

Corner and Dunlop (1997, p. 290) note that the 'trend towards medicalisation within palliative care deserves particular scrutiny since this is central to current debate surrounding the direction of the specialty'. Both Biswas (1993) and Field (1994) have observed in the British context, as I have done in the Australian setting, that palliative care has moved its emphasis from dying people to issues of symptom control and 'palliation', or the masking of the symptoms of dying. The issue of medicalisation goes hand in hand with what Clark (1993b) identifies as the development of a range of monoprofessional groups, somewhat paradoxically out of place with the hospice ethos of team work. It is not surprising that we find palliative medicine at the top of the hierarchy within the development of palliative care.

Medical dominance and the professionalisation of medical practice are common to the Western health care system (Freidson 1970a, 1970b;

Willis 1983, 1994; Daniels 1990). This dominance, which has an over-riding influence on the organisation of the health care system, is contingent upon the building of a body of scientific rational knowledge in the form of a 'discipline' (Foucault 1972, 1973). I have discussed the association between medicine and the management of dying in detail in Chapter 6, but the point to be made here is that medicine is organised in such a manner that precedence is given to physical causes and treatments. Palliative care practitioners try to combine medical treatments within a holistic framework of 'total care'. However, psychological, social and spiritual components of care, while considered important, are placed lower in the hierarchy of care. It is not surprising that the physical component of care is always placed first and that medicine is seen as the primary means of alleviating suffering.

> Mind–body dualism is so basic to Western culture that holistic or psychosomatic medical approaches are assimilated to it rather than resulting in any reform of practice. Distress is dichotomised into physical and mental, real and imaginary, accident and moral choice. The duality of mind and body expresses a tension between the unlimited world of thought and the finitude of bodily life. (Kirmayer 1988, p. 83)

The importance placed on medicine in the context of palliative care is seen in the establishment of the palliative medicine specialty and in the emphasis placed upon comparability of palliative care with other forms of medicine. The process of comparison then makes palliative care subject to the forms of bureaucracy associated with traditional medicine and health care.

SHIFTING PERSPECTIVES AND COMPETING VIEWS

Not all palliative care practitioners subscribe to the same views about the nature and future of palliative care. Many practitioners, particularly doctors and administrators, are determined to establish the credibility of palliative care as a legitimate and viable method of care for people suffering from diseases for which cure is highly improbable. These practitioners espouse methods which bring palliative care into line with mainstream health care services and professionalise the 'discipline' of palliative care through accreditation and evaluation combined with edu-cation, research and 'excellence' in clinical practice. By contrast many practitioners, particularly nurses, fear the changing focus of hospice and palliative care from broadly based holistic and supportive terminal care to a practice of symptomatology and, possibly, to an exercise in empire building amongst an elite group of specialists. There are those within this second group who may be involved in various elements of palliative care education and research and wish palliative care to be available to all dying patients, yet who sense that with the professionalisation of the 'discipline' has come a certain degree of medicalisation. A third group of practitioners, most often general practitioners who take on specialised palliative care work, or nurses who simply work their shifts in an inpatient hospice or domiciliary service, do not see themselves as part of a broader political enterprise and go about their daily work of caring for dying people. However, even these practitioners are influenced by the broader trends when they are asked to change their approaches to treatment or when they are prevented from providing psychosocial and supportive care due to the administrative and bureaucratic duties required of them.

The practitioners who are anxious to establish the credibility of palliative care cover a broad group of men and women; some are very politically motivated, while others almost naively believe that making palliative care more professional will mean that patient care will automatically be improved. Gordon, a palliative care doctor/medical specialist, said:

> One of my very strong themes that I like to let people know about is the credibility of palliative medicine as a speciality, not some crazy sideline thing that's mickey mouse or substandard clinically. In the past we tended to go along with the anecdotes, to say: 'Well this will do.' It's simply not good enough any more. We've got to match, if not better, what other specialties are doing.

Anne, a palliative care nurse and quality assurance officer, remarked:

> We were babes in the wood when we first started all those years ago, it's a bit horrifying to think about what we did in terms of documentation and treatment. I think we have got much more professional. Palliative care itself has changed. There's a lot more technology involved now . . . I've stopped using the catch phrase, 'You know, oh I really enjoy working in palliative care. There's nothing you can do wrong because they are all dying anyway.' . . . I think, for me, there are certain things that I thought were too invasive, but I've learnt that you really do have to keep an open mind . . . I think we've achieved a lot of credibility with the rest of the medical world.

While the need to be credible has acted as a strong motivating factor in the development of palliative care, some practitioners have expressed reservations which range from simple disillusionment to more direct criticism. Angie, a palliative care nurse, decided to leave 'hospice work' because she felt the 'tone' of the hospice had changed. Where once she believed her job entailed really caring for dying people and their families in a supportive environment, she now felt the hospice was 'on show, forever conscious that it is seen to be doing the right thing . . . we seem to change for change's sake.'

Vivienne, a palliative care nurse/administrator, noted:

> The challenge to the medical staff these days is how can we treat that symptom, so they are trying really to cure the symptom. And when they talk about getting the patient symptom free I think that the emphasis now has just gone too far—that they can justify using the most expensive technology, the most complex procedures and very expensive drugs on the basis that we are treating the symptoms. Somehow we have crossed over and we have lost sight of what true palliation in terminal illness is all about.

Sandy, a palliative care clinical nurse specialist, lamented:

> I try to go to a lot of the meetings which are concerned with policy directions and so forth. And what I see in the collectivity, you know all the health professionals involved, is a growing sense of power play, a great deal of castle building and competitiveness, particularly from the medicos. This form of medicalisation stops others from getting in to the patients to provide care. I just think we are going backwards.

For a large group of practitioners who constitute the palliative care 'workforce', rather than the political, administrative and educational leaders, translating the 'philosophy' into daily practice may be a personal challenge which is filtered through a number of bureaucratic procedures. These may range from changing policies regarding criteria for admission and the use of new technologies to changes in educational qualifications and accreditation. John, a palliative care doctor/general practitioner, describes how problems may present themselves in the form of criteria for patient admission to palliative care services, or even in the way that palliative care is defined and applied to daily practice:

> You know the criteria for admission have always been a bit nebulous. After ten years I'm not sure what these criteria are. I suppose it depends on how you feel at the time . . .

Richard, a palliative care doctor/general practitioner, believes that the ground is constantly shifting beneath the practitioners:

> There has been a big shift from the philosophy of three or four years ago, particularly in our increasing use of antibiotics, and intravenous lines . . . we would have considered them invasive then. Working on the suggestion that we follow the patient's options is reasonable and not necessarily against palliative care principles. Levels of intervention have to be negotiable . . . but this all takes up team resources.

These comments reflect the changes occurring within the palliative care community—exciting and challenging for some practitioners, though unsettling and disturbing for others as Dawn, a palliative care nurse/academic, remarked:

> It would be wonderful to know what we are really doing, to be able to describe ourselves, to find out what this is all about instead of just going about and doing it and not really realising the consequences.

MOVING PALLIATIVE CARE INTO THE MAINSTREAM

> There's actually a process of integration of palliative care services into mainstream services . . . a high degree of professionalism is required in order to achieve this. A number of specialists will be required for the foreseeable future, particularly in large teaching centres, as a means to an end and not as an end in themselves (Martin, palliative care doctor/medical specialist).

Martin believes that palliative 'approaches' should be used by all health professionals for people with incurable conditions, and that specialist teams should provide specialist services when required. The distinction between the palliative approach and specialist palliative care has also been noted in Britain (Finlay & Jones 1995; Clark & Seymour 1999). Ahmedzai (1997) extends these ideas by proposing that palliative care could be renamed as 'supportive care' or 'mixed management'. He suggests that this better reflects the focus on symptom control during advanced incurable illness. In this sense, palliative care should be seen as 'an adjunct, rather than an alternative, to other specialties, contributing its expertise in pain management, symptom control and family support' (Maddocks 1999, p. 64). However, this is not as straightforward as it seems and, as James and Field (1992) comment in the British context, the dialectical processes which take place between the 'hospices' and the mainstream health services need to be considered. These include reprofessionalisation of hospice (palliative) care, evaluation and audit, and financing and resourcing of the care. Not only does palliative care impact upon mainstream health services, but palliative care—and most particularly hospice—is changed in the process, and there is a very real possibility that the founding ideals of the hospice movement may be lost in the process.

Many of the important improvements in terminal care and advanced incurable illnesses have been prompted by the work done within the original hospice movement. Relief of pain and other distressing symptoms, and supportive care for families in their homes have been consistent goals of palliative care, which, on many occasions, have been met by services forced to be accountable to health care bureaucrats motivated by rationalist ideologies and policies. However, health care professionals who work within the mainstream services that claim to offer palliative care have other motivations which are sometimes perceived to be more competitive with, than complementary to, palliative care ideals. This broader perspective on palliative care may not include an acceptance and an openness to dying and death.

> I have a feeling that the oncology and the haematology, radiotherapy people see themselves as being able to provide palliative care . . . I feel as though it's almost watered down . . . I guess that our experience is that the philosophy of palliative care isn't transferring that well, as a complete package. You can teach the clinical side, but the approach of anticipating before you're immersed in the situation of total death and dying, giving people options earlier to opt out of certain treatment regimes, they are some of the things that don't happen. People can still provide good pain relief and symptom management and still have the family discussions without actually dealing with some of the issues that don't get addressed. The dilemma is that the people in the oncology area are still in a curative mode . . . it is still a frequent occurrence that we get people who have been treated until days, if not hours, of death from those very units who propose that they offer palliative care (Anna, palliative care nurse).

Some oncologists may prefer to administer their own kind of palliative care, which focuses on combining curative and palliative modes. This style of care may include counselling, but does not necessarily use the skills of a multidisciplinary palliative care team. Harry, an oncologist, insisted he could deliver palliative care as well as anyone, suggesting 'the trouble with most palliative care doctors is they want to introduce palliative care at birth'. Tensions obviously exist and the delivery of palliative care, at least within certain contexts, can become an item on a political agenda which involves competitiveness between medical specialities.

Many palliative care practitioners propose that palliative care should be available to all people who require good symptom management and support during the course of their terminal illness. Some practitioners who have been part of a palliative care community for some time may even share a common missionary focus. Margaret, an experienced palliative care nurse, believes:

> What we should be doing with palliative care is changing the health care system so it doesn't matter where you are dying—in the local nursing home, in a hostel, in a hospice, or in a hospital, because we have so communicated the ethos, the philosophy, the principles, and the knowledge and skill has been universally developed—not

specialised, but universally developed—then people will get good care
when they die. And that's the bottom line, people getting good care.

However, the translation of the hospice and palliative care ethos is a
complex process.

If you look at the nursing homes and at chronic disabled patients—there
you find a different view of palliative care to the one I hold . . . those
of us who see ourselves as doing the death and dying stuff . . . I'm
sure that it's got something to do with funding, there is funding available
for palliative care so now lots of organisations are keen to show that
they are providing palliative care even though it's as though they are
calling palliative care something else (Sue, palliative care clinical nurse
specialist).

The translation of the palliative care ethos appears most problematic
when palliative care is taken out of the traditional 'cancer model'.
Palliative care has developed in response to death by cancer where people
were expected to die within a relatively predictable period of time (Field
1996; Field & Addington-Hall 1999). Other non-malignant disease trajectories are not as predictable, so it is difficult to know when preparation
for death should begin, and in many cases these discussions do not take
place. Where doctors have learnt to give patients the 'bad news' about
their cancer, this communication pattern has not necessarily been transferred to other terminal conditions. Providing palliative care to people
with non-malignant terminal conditions may mean they receive good
symptom control and supportive care, but they may not necessarily be
socialised to death awareness and acceptance.

ESTABLISHING THE CREDIBILITY OF PALLIATIVE CARE

According to many practitioners, if palliative care is to be transferred to
mainstream practices, it must be judged by the standards acceptable to
the health department and must be comparable to other mainstream
services. This kind of credibility establishes palliative care as a competitive
force within the economic and political milieu of Australian health and
medical care. Palliative care has often been viewed as 'soft' and lacking
in intellectual rigour (MacDonald 1993, p. 65), and in need of earning
'the respect it so seeks' (Doyle 1993, p. 225).

Palliative care must go through the process of hardening up. We've got
to stop sounding soppy and start using objective language. We've got
to know the philosophy and start trying to live it in view of the current
health system. What we need is credibility and acceptability in the
mainstream health care (Angela, palliative care nurse/administrator).

However, it is often not possible to apply standard principles of evaluation to palliative care services, as Greg, a palliative care quality assurance officer, notes:

> Palliative care services can't be judged by the number of people who pass through the service to be returned to the community as well and productive members of society. It's difficult to put a value on time spent listening to patients or counselling family members, but they're supposed to be integral components to good palliative care . . . all the same the bottom line is the dollar.

The struggles to assure funding for palliative care are set firmly within the context of the ever-changing and rationalist discourses evident within the health care system. It is notable that, within this broader economic and political context, the strengthening and consolidation of medicine have been proposed as ways of establishing the credibility of palliative care. Where medicine has always been important to the overall context of palliative care, it now takes the central place in the development of the discipline.

There is now a developing medical focus evident within research and education in palliative care. The development of a body of specialised knowledge, together with the development of policies based on health needs assessments, can ultimately improve the quality of patient care (Robbins 1997; Hearn & Higginson 1998; Wilkinson et al. 1999). Nevertheless, other research acknowledges the difficulty of devising satisfactory measurement tools in order to demonstrate outcomes (Salisbury et al. 1999). In addition, the evidence-based model presently in favour in general medicine does not readily accommodate the patient-centred approach of palliative care (Wiffen 1998). It is important to acknowledge that the development of a body of clinical knowledge serves as the intellectual core of the political process whereby palliative medicine competes as a force within mainstream biomedical culture. Some practitioners, such as Janet, a palliative care nurse/administrator, believe that the social model of the original hospice movement has been replaced by expensive clinical specialties:

> I don't think that enough people in palliative care are looking at it as a social model . . . the major mission of hospice and palliative care is to change the health care system, it is not to create a system in its own right to be sustained for its own sake . . . I think we are going to see all palliative care services then fighting for the dollar as we fought for the dollars in the beginning to care for people who are terminally ill and we know that in the acute care system the dying patient never got value for money, because of these very same attitudes we see now in hospice palliative care.

Janet's reflections about the interrelationship between changing the health care system and the creation of a system in its own right highlight the problematic basis of the two themes of dissemination and credibility evident in palliative care practice. For many practitioners, these themes are accepted and are not necessarily open to scrutiny, while others are very aware of the changes taking place.

It appears that the team emphasis of palliative care, in particular the task ambiguity and the 'blurred or altered traditional patterns of hierarchy' evident in the early hospice approach (James & Field 1992, p. 1369), are being replaced by the leadership and the authority of the medical practitioner.

> The advent of medical and nursing specialisation means that entry criteria need to be set, and this may exclude many excellent health workers with diverse skills. Exclusion or admission criteria will narrow the field of expertise to doctors in academically based medicine and this means the focus upon palliative care education has the danger of inadvertently focusing on the symptoms and not the individual with the symptoms. Specialisation may also have the effect of making the palliative care movement a hierarchical structure of specialists, non-specialists, professionals and volunteers, rather than a team. (Mark, palliative care doctor)

As Mark suggests, the medically dominated hierarchy is orchestrated through the professionalisation of the discipline. Palliative care then simply mimics the hierarchical structures evident in traditional medicine and mainstream health care. For Janet, a palliative care nurse/administrator, this can mean that the 'clinical focus' changes the nature of the patient–practitioner encounter as well as the preparation for death associated with the palliative care ethos:

> I believe the team aspect is crucial to the missionary focus and I believe that it is being eroded . . . we need to have an inter-disciplinary focus and this need not be doctor led . . . What is palliative care supposed to be about? By homing in on the clinical aspects, you can lose track of where the patient has been, and where they might be in the progression of making up their mind . . . I do believe you need to understand that thread . . . we need to understand the bigger picture.

CONCLUSION

With the trends in palliative care indicating a greater level of medical intervention and hierarchical organisation, the original hospice vision which sought to reorient society to a greater acceptance of death could well be undermined. Jeffrey, a palliative care medical specialist, suggests that palliative care practitioners have a 'twisted psychology whereby they push death away . . . I sometimes wonder if palliative care work is a death-denying phenomenon.' Rose, a palliative care social worker, also believes that palliative care is a death-defying struggle: 'Palliative care is all about power, power over death.' Within the microcosm of palliative care, these comments may refer to the personal motivations of individual practitioners who challenge dying and death by having to face terminally ill people on a daily basis. However, 'denial of death' and 'power over death' are strong philosophical themes which are taken up in the discourse of medicine and death. In contrast to this power over death, the original hospice movement focused on the awareness and acceptance of death and, through this acceptance, a commitment to improving the care of dying people. Palliative care and palliative medicine still continue to have a commitment to improving the care of dying people, but the recognition of death is now often subtle, rather than explicit. Somehow this recognition is pushed into the background while practitioners attend to the physical needs of the patient. Where hospice originally sought to reorient the medical management of dying towards an acknowledgment of a good death, the awareness of dying is now once more masked by the complexities of suffering and dying in a contemporary society which is frenetically oriented to health, beauty and youth.

Dying and death are social processes and social problems, but they are 'managed' within the context of medicine, and as Kleinman (1995, p. 16) notes, the relationship between the social and the medical is not straightforward:

> What difference does it make—for theory, for research, for policy, and for societal ethics—to change the border between a social and a health problem? Now pulling the edge towards the social side, later on pushing it toward the medical margin—does that disclose a comparative advantage for 'medicalisation' of human misery under certain conditions, or for 'socialisation' under others? The moral, political, and the medical are culturally interrelated, but how do we best interpret that relationship and its implications?

While it is inevitable that the original hospice 'vision' will change and that the social movement will temper in accordance with dominant ideologies and practices, some practitioners express a sense of loss and an urgency to establish a balance between medicine and care.

> There is always the tension between the philosophy and ideals of caring for someone who is dying and the realities of care because you have to do some things for the person physically, but to me the secret, in the future, is going to be finding that balance. The scales have gone

out of balance . . . the doctors have become so involved and have seen it as a medical challenge, not as an issue about people's quality of life or about people dying as whole human beings resolving philosophical issues . . . What we have got to do, is hold on to the best clinical practice within a model of care which takes notice of the quality of the psychosocial and spiritual issues and also the morality of access and utilisation and distribution of resources (Vivienne, palliative care nurse/administrator).

Vivienne's words echo the sentiment expressed by Kleinman (1995), who stresses how the moral, political and the medical are culturally interrelated. This relationship is fraught with difficulty, yet—as Vivienne and many other palliative care practitioners acknowledge—it is only through critique of existing processes, and awareness of the problems at different levels, that change for the better can continue.

Hospice and palliative care appear, at present, to represent an area of contested ideas and practices which focus around the moral question of how best to die? Yet, paradoxically, the focus has shifted from the question of dying well to the problem of living well (even until death). Not only should patients live well (while dying), they should also be given reign to choose or refuse certain treatments and therapies that may improve their life and ultimately their death. However, these choices are constrained by a number of social and cultural dimensions which are often overlooked. An ideological framework is constructed to maintain the value of a 'good life' and this is facilitated through the medical control of 'symptoms'. This means that the hospice 'good death', as I also argue in Chapter 4, is an outdated concept. Socialisation to death, or to the gradual social death, has become unfashionable. Just as members of Western contemporary society are expected to age well with the aid of medical technology and a youthful spirit, dying people are expected to live well until they die. Death, surely, is part of life, as the hospice philosophy maintains—but an inevitable and embarrassing part of life, rather than a celebration and a focus of social life. In different historical periods and in different cultures, death has been accepted as fate and as a path to heaven, where today in dying, in caring for dying people and even in thinking about death, we acknowledge the dreadful uncertainty that underlies our fragile lives.

Methodological Appendix

The research that informs this book draws on a number of techniques, though primarily it is formulated within the anthropological tradition of ethnographic method. Ethnographers can be frustratingly vague when requested to provide details of what they do. This may be because the method of ethnography cannot be separated from the business of daily living. Traditionally ethnographers went to live with the people they studied and they immersed themselves in the culture of 'their people' in order to understand how those people lived. Ethnographers who study in urban communities still use this method of immersion. While they may return to their homes after the day's work, they do not altogether disengage from the question they wish to explore. They continue to pursue their research interests in an opportunistic fashion. All of the information they gather, in the varied contexts of contemporary society, is incorporated into the final production of the written text. The ethnography is both the means and the ends and the ethnographer is the research tool.

As with much of the more traditionally oriented ethnographic research, mine is not neatly packaged with strictly delimited borders of design, beginnings and endings. Most of the data that I present are taken from specific research sites during a limited time. Yet these data are informed by a number of both personal and professional experiences. From a personal perspective, some five years prior to my research, I had experienced palliative care first hand when my father died of cancer in a Palliative Care Unit. At the time of my later fieldwork I did not consciously link this experience to my professional endeavour other than to use it opportunistically to establish my credibility and level of understanding with the health professionals with whom I worked. However, upon reflection I believe this omission was not necessarily a determined, if somewhat outdated strategy, aimed at avoiding subjectivity in a supposed scientific investigation. Rather, my experience seemed of a different world, imprinted with the memory of pain and indifferent to the philosophical and organisational nature of the hospice. It has alerted me to the possibility that a family, like mine, may not share with palliative care practitioners similar understandings of the care given and received.

THE FIELDWORK: COMMUNITY AND SETTING

An interest in medical anthropology and health sociology stimulated my early research with the Western Australian palliative care community, which investigated, among other topics, the good death and stress and coping amongst palliative care nurses in both domiciliary and inpatient settings. This initial research was conducted over three months in 1993–94 and during this time I interviewed 22 experienced nurses aged between 25 and 62 years; half of these nurses were interviewed on a second occasion. The interviews, lasting between one and two and a half hours, followed an open-ended format whereby I responded to cues provided by the informants. However, some general questions were formulated as thematic and theoretical areas of concern arose and these were subsequently incorporated into the continuing inquiry. Nurses were encouraged to talk about their perceptions of the good death as well as to explain the procedures involved in 'good' palliative and terminal care. They were asked to relate stories of what they considered to be both 'good' and 'bad' deaths and to detail the part they played in these stories.

Participant observation complemented the interviewing techniques and this included attendance at staff and clinical team meetings, seminars and nursing handovers. Working with nurses in both inpatient and community settings and talking informally with nurses in staff rooms helped me to establish rapport and credibility. Participating with nurses in the 'hands on' care of patients, during both day and night shifts, provided me with the opportunity to share in some of the daily institutional concerns of the hospice environments and to observe the nurses' interactions with patients, families and colleagues including other nurses, doctors and administrative staff. Informal contact with nurses particularly provided an interactive forum in which to validate my observations and interpretations.

In 1995 I returned to conduct a more extensive ethnography of Western Australian palliative care services, although in the time that had elapsed between the two periods of fieldwork I maintained contact through professional and informal activities involved in research, publication and education. The initial period of ethnographic fieldwork, in which I became interested in the concept of the good death, also alerted me to a rapid evolution of ideas and practices within the Western Australian palliative care community. I saw that many of the new thoughts and forms had the potential both to undermine and support traditional medical practices concerning dying and death. In this second period of fieldwork, conducted between May 1995 and July 1996, I attempted to include a more diverse range of participants, including doctors, nurses, counsellors and other allied health professionals, volunteers, chaplains and other spiritual support staff, and patients and their families. Most of the formal fieldwork was conducted in two settings, the palliative care community service and the 26 bed, free-standing inpatient hospice (including a purpose-built day hospice) where I had conducted earlier fieldwork. The patient profile of the hospice features a mix of respite (short-stay), acute care and patients who are admitted for terminal care.

Although most of the data gathered for my study, and for this book, came from fairly specific field sites, the final ethnography exists as the cumulative experience with the palliative care community over four years. During that time I gathered large amounts of information which exist in various forms. I spent approximately four months visiting eight metropolitan bases of an integrated palliative care community service. This time was spent in attending clinical meetings and talking with the multidisciplinary teams at the bases; interviewing nurses, doctors, chaplains, counsellors and care aides; and accompanying nurses as they visited patients and families in four of the metropolitan bases. Observation, informal interaction and interviews with multidisciplinary team members were conducted over four months in the inpatient hospice. During this time I accompanied nurses, doctors, an occupational therapist and a social worker as they cared for patients and, in some cases, the patients' families and friends. I attended various kinds of meetings, ward rounds and nursing handovers in which the patients' care and clinical management, as well as issues of general policy, were discussed.

In both of the fieldwork settings I employed various ethnographic strategies in order to validate my observations, especially in relation to what I was told or what I had heard others say. On some occasions I subsequently interviewed the person with whom I had worked, while at other times I accompanied practitioners on repeated work shifts or spent time with different team members who were involved in the management of the same patients. These various strategies were essentially opportunistic. During the period from May 1995 to July 1996, I accompanied 32 health professionals while they worked. I spent many hours of observation with all of these professionals, though I found that some particularly enjoyed the experience and allowed me to accompany them for several repeated work shifts. In the period from May 1995 to January 1997, I conducted 52 interviews which were generally open-ended and of a duration of at least one hour. While these details give some indication of the time spent in observation and interviewing, I stress that the ethnographic approach is ongoing and often informal. Some of my most valuable data were collected serendipitously. For example, I had several telephone conversations with two external students who were studying a unit I taught. Both were hospice nurses and were very eager to talk to me about their experiences. On another occasion I sat next to a hospice nurse on an aeroplane and had a lengthy and valuable talk. Many hours were spent in the lunch room at the inpatient hospice and many more again with domiciliary nurses as we drove from one patient's home to the next. While I am mindful of the ethical nature of my work and have not included quotes or observations where I have not had written consent to do so, these broader experiences have informed my understanding of the changing context of medical and palliative care practices in contemporary Australia. During another period of fieldwork, encompassing approximately four months, I visited several other Western Australian hospice and palliative care services, observed meetings and conducted more formal interviews with various health professionals, chaplains and administrators, most notably at a large teaching hospital. I have also spent time in a large Western Australian country centre, which has a free-standing hospice, palliative care appointed beds in the local hospital and a consultant hospice nurse who works through the domiciliary nursing service.

Although my research has focused mainly on health professionals who care for terminally ill people and their families, I have, in the course of my work, spoken to a large number of dying people and their families. During my initial ethnographic research I did not formally interview patients and family members but I did help to move, feed and wash patients and I made beds and cups of tea; I helped, in my limited way, to dress wounds and prepare dead bodies, sat in the garden with relatives and friends and generally witnessed what has often seemed like unbearable grief. More recently, I have conducted a study of ethnic diversity in dying, death and bereavement and, with another researcher, interviewed 53 people who were either terminally ill themselves, a close relative of a terminally ill person, or a bereaved person. As an indication of the ethnic and cultural diversity of the local population we found that simply by interviewing suitable people over a period of four months, we managed to speak with people from 22 different ethnic backgrounds. My participation in professional meetings of various kinds (both academic and those related to palliative care) has given me the opportunity to visit various hospices and palliative care services as well as to interview a number of people in different parts of the world. My experiences in Singapore, Hong Kong and China, as well as my more extensive visits to various locations in South Australia and New South Wales, have informed my observations about the way that dying is managed in a palliative care context.

THE ETHNOGRAPHIC CYCLE AND THE PROCESS OF ANALYSIS

With the ethnographic cycle, proposed by Spradley (1980, p. 28–9), the process of research is ongoing and continually subject to change. Certain elements of the pattern of data collection are repeated over and over again and are open to modification. Analysis of the data occurs at the same time as data collection and influences further data collection. Explanations that are tentatively offered are tested out and used to develop theory, which will then be tested out again in the research site. The anomaly will prompt the researcher to look again, and the un-intentioned 'mistake', rather than ruining the research design, may lead to new and productive enquiries. The ethnographer observes, evaluates, retraces, crosschecks by using various strategies, and then re-evaluates. Skill is needed in establishing rapport, observing and listening. I found, as an ethnographer, my presentation of self was important in establishing trust and credibility, as was my willingness to wait and listen empathically. Often, the ethnographic method can be a lengthy process with hours spent 'hanging around' so that the participants of the study are so used to the presence of the ethnographer that they do not stop to question why he or she is present.

Analysis in the ethnographic cycle occurs concurrently with data collection. In the course of my fieldwork I constantly noted themes, made focused observations and developed strategies based upon these themes which I cross-referenced in personal journals and fieldnotes. In the early stages of the fieldwork the interpretation is undeveloped and occasionally based upon 'hunches' which are gradually supported as more and more data begin to reinforce the 'hunch' or the 'felt experience'. With any kind of qualitative research 'doing the work is like slaughtering a pig, as the Italians say: "You don't throw anything away"' (Eco cited in and translated by Schratz & Walker, 1995 p. 126).

OTHER METHODOLOGICAL ISSUES

My ethnographic exploration of how dying and death are understood in local settings draws upon sociological analysis which 'occurs in micro-interactional contexts, between professionals and patients, but these interactions are shaped partly by discourses and goals belonging to (and shaping) macro-institutional and organisational contexts' (Costain Schou 1993, p. 238). The methodological emphasis requires that both levels be seen as private and public elements of a broader discourse about dying and death (Prior 1989), but also, particularly, in relation to biomedical practice and the construction of biomedical knowledge. I consider biomedicine to be a cultural system and I attempt to demonstrate the interdependence of biomedicine, society and culture. With this overarching aim I use various descriptions and direct quotes from informants to show how values, language, metaphor, ritual and institutional practices contribute to contemporary ideas and beliefs about the care of dying people and the medical management of death. My ethnographic approach goes beyond the 'etic' which seeks to describe and evaluate an object of interest, to incorporate the 'emic' frame of analysis which focuses on subject-centred sources of data (Hughes 1992, p. 445). Various forms of data are consequently gathered and analysed in different ways. I have drawn from extensive fieldnotes, a few of which have existed from earlier research and lend themselves again to a re-reading, confirming that data are not fixed (Atkinson 1992); strategic interviews have been transcribed while conversations engaged in and overheard have been noted as carefully as possible; and various texts from local agencies, government organisations and palliative care journals lend themselves to a more literary analysis. One intention, among many others, is to describe, in ethnographic fashion, the lived experiences of dying people, their families, friends and professional carers.

Ethnographic research involves detailed descriptive accounts and I have set these accounts of death, dying and care within 'local worlds' which encompass a social network in which actions have cultural, political, economic, institutional, and social relational sources and consequences (Kleinman 1992, p.128). Kleinman's concept of local worlds provides the ethnographer with a framework which gives some shape and coherence even to fragmented and contested local contexts. It also allows the ethnographer to view interpersonal experience from afar in order to describe and possibly compare other local worlds and local ways of being human. Following this framework, I acknowledge lack of consensus or disagreement honestly and report variations when they appear within the groups of people I have studied; but more importantly, I draw sociological and cultural threads together to demonstrate familiar patterns which confirm our common humanity.

Conducting ethnographic research and writing an ethnographic account prove particularly challenging in the context of present day social science. Denizin (1996, p.127) tells us social science, with the other human disciplines, is confronted with a double crisis of representation and legitimation. This crisis has been attributed to the growing influence of postmodernism upon contemporary social theory (Ahmed & Shore 1995, p.14). Within anthropology, particularly, an 'uncertainty about adequate means of describing social reality' has cast doubts upon traditional scientific ethnography (Marcus & Fischer 1986, p.8). The epistemological status of ethnography has been called into question. As such, the ethnographer must account for: the existence of the empirical world; the knowability of other minds; and the validity of the ethnographic representation (Jessor 1996, p.8). I agree with Hastrup (1995, p.121), who believes that postmodernism need not lead to 'a dismissal of the possibility of obtaining objective knowledge about the real world'. This task however, eludes traditional concepts as the 'worlds' which researchers seek to investigate are plural and fragmented. And the people who inhabit the worlds create dynamic cultures by changing any so-called 'logical' patterns of ideas to suit their own contradictory and ambiguous purpose. If the minds of these people can be known, it is in a partial and historical way that can be managed by the researcher, given a certain amount of time (Agar 1996, p. 36). Ethnography can be done, although 'knowing the other is problematic' (Campbell 1996, p. 169). In order to do ethnography the issue of representation must be dealt with head on. Hammersly's proposition (1992, p. 2) that data could be a product of participation in the field rather than a reflection of the phenomenon studied must be considered. The issue of legitimation of data is one of practical epistemology which concerns 'how what we do affects the credibility of the propositions we advance' (Becker 1996, p. 57). In many ways the credibility of my account cannot be known until it resonates with some of the community of people it investigates. Yet verisimilitude and apparency, criteria for measuring the ethnographic account, can, in some sense, also be appreciated by other readers who are familiar with other contexts or with more theoretical aspects of the argument.

SURVEY DATA

I refer to two surveys in various chapters of this book. One survey (McNamara et al. 1997), which I have mentioned only briefly, involved approximately 200 palliative care practitioners (nurses, doctors, counsellors, allied health and spiritual support staff). These practitioners responded to a questionnaire that proposed three scenarios which described a patient and the circumstances surrounding their condition.

The focus of the questionnaire was to elicit responses regarding the care of ethnically diverse patients who all had varying needs, some of which related to lack of English speaking skills and cultural beliefs. The respondents were asked to rate their perceived competence in delivering care for each scenario and to provide details about their levels of training and experience. Other questions focused on the perceived difficulty of specific issues that related to care; for example, the ability to assess the patient and aspects of communication such as discussing the diagnosis and prognosis. Through this study, I was able to demonstrate, with my co-authors, that palliative care practitioners feel significantly less competent in caring for people from ethnic backgrounds that are very different from their own. These observations have informed my understandings of how the care of dying people is both complicated and enriched through the diversity of Western multicultural societies.

I have used data from a second survey (Waddell & McNamara 1997) of a sample of the Australian population to analyse beliefs about facing death, focusing specifically on advanced directives and euthanasia. Approximately 370 Anglo Australians and 90 Chinese Australians responded to a questionnaire which asked how they would want to be treated if they had a life-threatening irreversible illness. More details about the kinds of questions asked are given in Chapter 2, 'Thoughts about facing death'. By contrasting the results of this survey with qualitative data from interviews with terminally ill people and their families, I have been able to illustrate the important point that people often change their minds about important issues like euthanasia when they are close to death. In other words, it is far more common to advocate a general belief in the principle of euthanasia than to request a medically assisted death. Both surveys I refer to use relatively small samples due to the size of the Western Australian population and of the local palliative care community. However, I believe many of the issues raised in the analysis reflect findings from other researchers and I have illustrated many of these connections in my extensive review of literature from various Western societies.

References

Abel, E 1986, 'The hospice movement: institutionalising innovation', *International Journal of Health Services*, vol. 16, no. 1, pp. 71–85

Addington-Hall, J, Altman, D & McCarthy, M 1998, 'Which terminally ill cancer patients receive hospice in-patient care?', *Social Science and Medicine*, vol. 46, no. 8, pp. 1011–16

Agar, M 1996, *The Professional Stranger: An Informal Introduction to Ethnography*, Academic Press, San Diego

Ahmed, A & Shore, C 1995, 'Introduction: is anthropology relevant to the contemporary world?' in *The Future of Anthropology: Its Relevance to the Contemporary World*, eds A Ahmed & C Shore, Athlone, London & Atlantic Highlands

Ahmedzai, S 1997, 'New approaches to pain control in patients with cancer', *European Journal of Cancer*, vol. 33, suppl. 6, pp. S8–S14

Anderson, R 1996, *Magic, Science and Health: The Aims and Achievements of Medical Anthropology*, Harcourt Brace College Publishers, Fort Worth

Aneshensel, C 1992, 'Social stress: theory and research', *Annual Review of Sociology*, vol. 18, pp. 15–38

Anonymous 1997, 'Last Rights', in *Economist*, vol. 343, no. 8022, pp. 21–4

Aries, P 1974, *Western Attitudes to Death*, John Hopkins University Press, Baltimore

——1981, *The Hour of Our Death*, Allen Lane, London

Armstrong, D 1987, 'Silence and truth in death and dying', *Social Science and Medicine*, vol. 24, no. 8, pp. 651–7

Ashby, M & Wakefield, M 1993, 'Attitudes to some aspects of death, dying, living wills and substituted health care decision-making in South Australia: public opinion survey for a parliamentary select committee', *Palliative Medicine*, vol. 7, no. 4, pp. 273–82

Astrom, G, Jansson, L, Norberg, A & Hallberg, R 1993, 'Experienced nurses' narratives of their being in ethically difficult care situations', *Cancer Nursing*, vol. 16, no. 3, pp. 179–87

Athlin, E, Furaker, C, Jansson, L & Norberg, A 1993, 'Application of primary nursing within a team setting in the hospice care of cancer patients', *Cancer Nursing*, vol. 16, no. 5, pp. 388–97

Atkinson, P, 1992, 'The ethnography of a medical setting: reading, writing, and rhetoric', Qualitative Health Research, vol. 2, no. 4, pp. 451–74

——1995, *Medical Talk and Medical Work*, Sage, London

Atkinson, T, Liem, R, & Liem, J 1986, 'The social costs of unemployment: implications for social support', *Journal of Health and Social Behaviour*, vol. 27, pp. 317–31

Australian Bureau of Statistics 1997 Unpublished data provided on place of death in Western Australia for 1995

——2000, 'Australia Now—A Statistical Profile', http://www.abs.gov.au/websitedbs/

Badham, P 1996, 'Life and death in the light of an eternal hope', in *Facing Death: An Interdisciplinary Approach,* eds. P Badham & P Ballard, University of Wales Press, Cardiff

Ballard, P 1992, 'The ethnography of a medical setting: reading, writing, and rhetoric', *Qualitative Health Research,* vol. 2, no. 4, pp. 451–74

——1996, 'Intimations of mortality: some sociological considerations', in *Facing Death: An Interdisciplinary Approach,* eds. P Badham & P Ballard, University of Wales Press, Cardiff

Balshem, M 1991, 'Cancer, control, and causality: talking about cancer in a working-class community', *American Ethnologist*, vol. 18, no. 1, pp. 152–73

Bates, E & Lapsley, H 1985, *The Health Machine: The Impact of Medical Technology*, Penguin, Ringwood

Bauman, Z 1992, *Mortality, Immortality and Other Life Strategies*, Polity Press, Cambridge

Baume, P 1993, 'Living and dying: a paradox of medical progress', *The Medical Journal of Australia*, vol. 159, no. 11–12, pp. 792–4

——1998, 'Voluntary euthanasia: responses of medical practitioners in NSW and the ACT to six open-ended questions', *Australian & New Zealand Journal of Public Health*, vol. 22, no. 2, pp. 269–70

Beck, U 1992, *Risk Society: Towards a New Modernity*, trans. M Ritter, Sage, London

Becker, H 1996, 'The epistemology of qualitative research', in *Ethnography and Human Development: Context and Meaning in Social Inquiry*, eds R Jessor, A Colby & R Shweder, The University of Chicago Press, Chicago

Benoliel, J 1983, 'Nursing research on death, dying and terminal illness: development, present state, and prospects', *Annual Review of Nursing Research*, vol. 1, pp. 101–30

Berger, P 1967, *The Sacred Canopy: Elements of a Sociological Theory of Religion*, Anchor Books, New York

Biswas, B 1993, 'The medicalization of dying: a nurse's view', in *The Future for Palliative Care: Issues of Policy and Practice*, ed. D Clark, Open University Press, Buckingham

Blauner, R 1966, 'Death and social structure', *Psychiatry*, vol. 29, no. 4, pp. 378–94

Bloch, M & Parry J eds 1982, *Death and the Regeneration of Life*, Cambridge University Press, Cambridge

Bradbury, M 1993, 'Contemporary representations of "good" and "bad" death', in *Death, Dying and Bereavement,* eds D Dickenson & M Johnson, Sage, London

——1996, 'Representations of "good" and "bad" death among deathworkers and the bereaved', in *Contemporary Issues on the Sociology of Death, Dying and Disposal*, eds. G Howarth & P Jupp, Macmillan, London

Bradshaw, A 1996, 'The spiritual dimension of hospice: the secularisation of an ideal', *Social Science and Medicine*, vol. 43, no. 3, pp. 409–19

Caddell, D & Newton, R 1995, 'Euthanasia: American attitudes toward the physician's role', *Social Science and Medicine*, vol. 40, no. 12, pp. 1671–81

Callahan, D 1993, *The Troubled Dream of Life: Living With Mortality*, Simon & Schuster, New York

Campbell, A 1990, 'An ethic for hospice', unpublished Conference paper presented at the Australian Hospice Palliative Care Conference, Adelaide, South Australia

Campbell, D 1996, 'Can we overcome worldview incommensurability/relativity in trying to understand the other?', in *Ethnography and Human Development: Context and Meaning in Social Inquiry*, eds R Jessor, A Colby & R Shweder, The University of Chicago Press, Chicago

Cassell, E 1975, 'Dying in a technological society', in *Death Inside Out: The Hastings Centre Report*, eds P Steinfels & R Veatch, Harper & Row, New York

Cassileth, B 1983, 'The evolution of oncology', *Perspectives in Biology and Medicine*, vol. 26, no. 3, pp. 362–74

Castle, N & Mor, V 1998, 'Advance care planning in nursing homes: pre-and post-*Patient Self Determination Act*', *Health Services Research*, vol. 33, no. 1, pp. 101–24

Charles, C, Gafni, A & Whelan, T 1999, 'Decision-making in the physician–patient encounter: revisiting the shared treatment', *Social Science and Medicine*, vol. 49, no. 5, pp. 651–61

Charmaz, K 1980, *The Social Reality of Death*, Addison-Wesley, Reading

Chater, S, Viola, R, Paterson, J & Jarvis, V 1998, 'Sedation for intractable distress in the dying—a survey of experts', *Palliative Medicine*, vol. 12, no. 4, pp. 255–69

Chen, E, David, A, Nunnerley, H, Michell, M, Dawson, J, Berry, H, Dobbs, J & Fahy, T 1995, 'Adverse life events and breast cancer: case control study', *British Medical Journal*, vol. 311, no. 7019, pp. 1527–30

Clapp, RW 1998, 'The decline in US cancer mortality from 1991 to 1995: what's behind the numbers?', *International Journal of Health Services*, vol. 24, no. 4, pp. 747–55

Clark, D 1991, 'Contradictions in the development of new hospices: a case study', *Social Science and Medicine*, vol. 33, no. 9, pp. 995–1004

——1993a, 'Introduction', in *The Sociology of Death*, ed. D Clark, Blackwell, Oxford

——1993b, 'Whither the hospices?', in *The Future of Palliative Care: Issues of Policy and Practice*, ed. D Clark, Open University Press, Buckingham

——1998, 'Originating a movement: Cicely Saunders and the development of St Christopher's Hospice, 1957–67', *Mortality*, vol. 3, no. 1, pp. 43–63

——1991, '"Total pain", disciplinary power and the body in the work of Cicely Saunders, 1958–67, *Social Science and Medicine*, vol. 49, no. 6, pp. 727–36

——1999b, 'Cradled to the Grave? Terminal care in the United Kingdom, 1948–67', *Mortality*, vol. 4, no. 3, pp. 225–47

Clark, D & Seymour, J 1999, *Reflections on Palliative Care: Sociological and Policy Perspectives*, Open University Press, Buckingham

Coates, A 1998, 'Cancer control in Australia', *The Medical Journal of Australia*, vol. 169, no. 1, pp. 8–9

Corner, J & Dunlop, R 1997, 'New approaches to care', in *New Themes in Palliative Care*, eds D Clark, J Hockley & S Ahmedzai, Open University Press, Buckingham

Corr, C & Corr, D 1983, *Hospice Care: Principles and Practice*, Faber and Faber, New York

Costain Schou, K 1993, 'Awareness contexts and the construction of dying in the cancer treatment setting: "micro" and "macro" levels in narrative analysis', in *The Sociology of Death*, ed. D Clark, Blackwell, Oxford

Costain Schou, K & Hewison, J 1999, *Experiencing Cancer: Quality of Life in Treatment*, Open University Press, Buckingham

Csordas, T 1990, 'Embodiment as a paradigm for anthropology', *Ethos*, vol. 18, no. 5, pp. 5–47

——ed. 1994, *Embodiment and Experience: The Existential Ground of Culture and Self*, Cambridge University Press, Cambridge

Daniel, A 1998, 'Trust and medical authority', in *Health Matters: A Sociology of Illness, Prevention and Care*, eds A Petersen & C Waddell, Allen & Unwin, Sydney

Daniels, A 1990, *Medicine and the State: Professional Autonomy and Public Accountability*, Allen & Unwin, Sydney

Danis, M, Federman, D, Fins, J, Fox, E, Kastenbaum, B, Lanken, P, Long, K, Lowenstein, E, Lynn, J, Rouse, F & Tulsky, J 1999, 'Incorporating palliative care into critical care education: principles, challenges, and opportunities', *Critical Care Medicine*, vol. 27, no. 9, pp. 2005–13

Davis, A & George, J 1993, *States of Health: Health and Illness in Australia*, 2nd edn, Harper Educational, Sydney

De Vaus, D 1996, 'Religious community', in *Social Self, Global Culture: An Introduction to Sociological Ideas*, ed. A Kellehear, Oxford University Press, Oxford

Des Aulniers, L 1993, 'The organisation of life before death in two Quebec cultural configurations', *Omega*, vol. 27, no. 1, pp. 35–50

DiGiacomo, S 1987, 'Biomedicine as a cultural system: an anthropologist in the kingdom of the sick', in *Encounters With Biomedicine*, ed. H Baer, Gordon & Breach Science Publishers, New York

Dodds, J 1997, Cancer as bad luck or warning symbol? Constructed meanings of illness and healing, PhD thesis, The University of Western Australia, Perth

Doyle, D 1992, 'Have we looked beyond the physical and the psychosocial?', *Journal of Pain and Symptom Management*, vol. 7, no. 5, pp. 302–11

——1993, 'Palliative medicine: a time for definition?', *Palliative Medicine*, vol. 7, no. 4, pp. 253–5

du Boulay, S 1984, *Cicely Saunders: The Founder of the Modern Hospice Movement*, Hodder & Stoughton, London

Edgar, A 1996, 'The importance of death in shaping our understanding of life', in *Facing Death: An Interdisciplinary Approach*, eds P Badham & P Ballard, University of Wales Press, Cardiff

Elias, N 1985, *The Loneliness of Dying*, Blackwell, Oxford

Enck, R 1993, 'The physician's view of hospice', *The American Journal of Hospice and Palliative Care*, vol. 10, no. 6, p. 1

Field, D 1989, *Nursing the Dying*, Tavistock/Routledge, London

——1994, 'Palliative medicine and the medicalization of death', *European Journal of Cancer Care*, vol. 3, no. 2, pp. 58–62

——1996, 'Awareness and modern dying', *Mortality*, vol. 1, no. 3, pp. 255–65

Field, D & Addington-Hall, J 1999, 'Extending specialist palliative care to all?', *Social Science and Medicine*, vol. 48, no. 9, pp. 1271–80

Field, D & Copp, G 1999, 'Communication and awareness about dying in the 1990s', *Palliative Medicine*, vol. 13, no. 6, pp. 459–68

Field, D & Johnson, I 1993, 'Volunteers in the British hospice movement', in *The Sociology of Death*, ed. D Clark, Blackwell, Oxford

Finlay, I 1996, 'Ethical decision-making in palliative care: the clinical reality' in *Facing Death: An Interdisciplinary Approach*, eds P Badham & P Ballard, University of Wales Press, Cardiff

Finlay, I & Jones, R 1995, 'Definitions in palliative care', *British Medical Journal*, vol. 311, no. 7007, p. 754

Foucault, M 1970, *The Order of Things: An Archaeology of the Human Sciences*, trans. AM Sheridan Smith, Tavistock, London

——1972, *The Archaeology of Knowledge*, trans. AM Sheridan Smith, Tavistock, London

——1973, *The Birth of the Clinic: An Archaeology of Medical Perception*, trans. AM Sheridan Smith, Tavistock, London

——1989, *Madness and Civilisation: A History of Insanity in the Age of Reason*, trans. R Howard, Routledge, London

——1991, 'The politics of health in the eighteenth century', in *The Foucault Reader*, ed. P Rainbow, Penguin, London

Fox, N 1993, *Postmodernism, Sociology and Health*, Open University Press, Buckingham

Frank, A 1999, 'The body as territory and as wonder', in *Health Studies: A Critical and Cross-Cultural Reader*, ed. C Samson, Blackwell, Oxford

Frank, G, Blackhall, L, Michel, V, Murphy, S, Azen, S & Park, K 1998, 'A discourse of relationships in bioethics: patient autonomy and end-of-life decision making among elderly Korean Americans', *Medical Anthropology Quarterly*, vol. 12, no. 4, pp. 403–23

Frankenberg, R 1992, '"Your time or mine": temporal contradictions of biomedical practice', in *Time, Health and Medicine*, ed. R Frankenberg, Sage, London

Freidson, E 1970a, *Professional Dominance*, Aldine, Chicago

——1970b, *Profession of Medicine: A Study of the Sociology of Applied Knowledge*, Dodd, Mead & Company, New York

Freund, P & McGuire M 1991, *Health, Illness, and the Social Body: A Critical Sociology*, Prentice Hall, Englewood Cliffs

Frey, D 1981, *Report to the Cancer Council of Western Australia on hospice feasibility: executive summary*, Division of Health Sciences for Advanced Studies, Western Australian Institute of Technology

Frontline, 1999 'The Kevorkian Verdict', http://www.pbs.org/wgbh/pages/frontline/kevorkian

Fulton, R ed. 1965, *Death and Identity*, Wiley, New York

Gavin, W 1995, *Cuttin' the Body Loose: Historical, Biological, and Personal Approaches to Death and Dying*, Temple University Press, Philadelphia

Geertz, C 1988, *Works and Lives. The Anthropologist as Author*, Stanford University Press, Stanford

Giddens, A 1990, *The Consequences of Modernity*, Polity Press, Cambridge

——1991, *Modernity and Self-Identity: Self and Society in the Late Modern Age*, Polity Press, Cambridge

Gilman, S 1995, *Health and Illness: Images of Difference*, Reaktion Books, London

Glaser, B & Strauss, A 1966, *Awareness of Dying*, Weidenfeld & Nicholson, London

——1968, *Time for Dying*, Aldine, Chicago

——1971, *Status Passage*, Routledge & Kegan Paul, London

Glick, H 1992, *The Right to Die: Policy Innovation and Its Consequences*, Columbia University Press, New York

Goffman, E 1963, *Stigma: Notes on the Management of Spoiled Identity*, Prentice-Hall, New Jersey

Good, B 1994, *Medicine, Rationality, and Experience: An Anthropological Perspective*, Cambridge University Press, Cambridge

Good, M, Good, B, Schaffer, C & Lind, S 1990, 'American oncology and the discourse of hope', *Culture, Medicine and Psychiatry*, vol. 14, no. 1, pp. 59–79

Good, M, Hunt, L, Munakata, T & Kobayashi, Y 1993, 'A comparative analysis of the culture of biomedicine: disclosure and consequences for treatment in the practice of oncology', in *Health and Health Care in Developing Countries*, eds P Conrad & E Gallagher, Temple University Press, Philadelphia

Goodlin, S 1997, 'What is palliative care?', *Hospital Practice*, vol. 32, no. 2, pp. 13–16

Gordon, D 1988, 'Tenacious assumptions in Western medicine', in *Biomedicine Examined*, eds M Lock & D Gordon, Kluwer Academic Publishers, Dordrecht

——1990, 'Embodying illness, embodying cancer', *Culture, Medicine and Psychiatry*, vol. 14, no. 2, pp. 275–97

Gordon, D & Paci, E 1997, 'Disclosure practices and narratives: understanding concealment and silence around cancer in Tuscany, Italy', *Social Science and Medicine*, vol. 44, no. 10, pp. 1433–52

Gorer, G 1955, 'The pornography of death', reprinted in G Gorer 1965, *Death, Grief, and Mourning in Contemporary Britain*, The Cresset Press, London

——1965, *Death, Grief, and Mourning in Contemporary Britain*, The Cresset Press, London

Government Statistical Service (UK) 1999, 'The UK in Figures: Population and Vital Statistics', http://www.statistics.gov.uk/stats/ukinfigs/pop.htm

Guadagnoli, E & Ward, P 1998, 'Patient participation in decision-making', *Social Science and Medicine*, vol. 47, no. 3, pp. 329–39

Hamil-Luker, J & Smith, C 1998, 'Religious authority and public opinion on the right to die', *Sociology of Religion*, vol. 59, no. 4, pp. 373–91

Hammer, M 1983, 'Core and extended social networks in relation to health and illness', *Social Science and Medicine*, vol. 17, no. 7, pp. 405–11

Hammersley, M 1992, *What's Wrong With Ethnography? Methodological Explorations*, Routledge, London

Hastrup, K 1995, 'The complexity of the present: ethical implications', in *Post-modernism and Anthropology: Theory and Practice*, eds K Geujen, D Raven & J de Wolf, Van Gorcum, Assen, The Netherlands

Hearn, J & Higginson, I 1998, 'Do specialist palliative care teams improve outcomes for cancer patients? A systematic review', *Palliative Medicine*, vol. 12, no. 5, pp. 317–32

Helme, T. 1992 'Euthanasia around the world', *British Medical Journal*, vol. 304, no. 6828, p. 717

Herzlich, C & Pierret, J 1987, *Illness and Self in Society*, John Hopkins University Press, Baltimore

Hertz, R 1960, *Death and the Right Hand*, trans. R Needham & C Needham, Cohen & West, Aberdeen

Hewitt, M 1996, 'Death on the net', *Link-up*, vol. 13, no. 4, p. 28

Hinds, P, Chaves, D & Cypess, S 1992, 'Context as a source of meaning and understanding', *Qualitative Health Research*, vol. 2, no. 1, pp. 61–74

Hockey, J 1996, 'The view from the West: reading the anthropology of non–western death ritual', in *Contemporary Issues in the Sociology of Death, Dying and Disposal*, eds G Howarth & P Jupp, Macmillan, London

——1997, 'Women in grief: cultural representation and social practice', in *Death, Gender and Ethnicity*, eds D Field, J Hockey & N Small, Routledge, London

Hockley, J 1999, 'Specialist palliative care within the acute hospital setting', *Acta Oncologica*, vol. 38, no. 4, pp. 491–4

Hospice Care Service: In Review 1993, Silver Chain Nursing Association, Perth, Western Australia

Huang, X, Butow, P, Meiser, B & Golstein, D 1999, 'Attitudes and information needs of Chinese migrant cancer patients and their relatives', *Australian and New Zealand Journal of Medicine*, vol. 29, no. 2, pp. 207–13

Hughes, C 1992, '"Ethography": what's in a word—process? product? promise?', *Qualitative Health Research*, vol. 2, no. 4, pp. 439–50

Humphry, D 1991, *Final Exit: The Practicalities of Self-Deliverance and Assisted Suicide for the Dying*, Penguin, Ringwood

Humphreys, S and King, H 1981, *Mortality and Immortality: the Anthropology and Archaeology of Death*, Academic Press, London

Hunsaker Hawkins, A 1991, 'Constructing death: three pathographies about dying', *Omega*, vol. 22, no. 4, pp. 301–17

Hunt, R 1994, 'Palliative care—the rhetoric–reality gap', in *Willing to Listen: Wanting to Die*, ed. H Kuhse, Penguin, Ringwood

Hunt, R, Maddocks, D, Roach, D & McLeod, A 1995, 'The incidence of requests for a quicker terminal course', *Palliative Medicine*, vol. 9, no. 2, pp. 167–8

Illich, I 1976, *Limits to Medicine. Medical Nemesis: The Expropriation of Health*, Marion Boyars, London

Jacobsen, G 1985, 'Hospice: what it is not', *Hospice Support Organisation of Western Australia Newsletter*, no. 11

Jacobson, D 1989, 'Context and the sociological study of stress: an invited response to Pearlin', *Journal and Health and Social Behaviour*, vol. 30, pp. 257–60

James, N 1989, 'Emotional labour: skill and work in the social regulation of feelings', *The Sociological Review*, vol. 37, pp. 15–42

James, N & Field, D 1992, 'The routinisation of hospice: charisma and bureaucratisation', *Social Science and Medicine*, vol. 34, no. 12, pp. 1363–75

James, V 1986 Care and work in nursing the dying: a participant study of a continuing care unit, unpublished PhD thesis, University of Aberdeen

Jessor, R 1996, 'Ethographic methods in contemporary perspective', in *Ethnography and Human Development: Context and Meaning in Social Inquiry*, eds R Jessor, A Colby & R Shweder, The University of Chicago Press, Chicago

Kastenbaum, R 1977, *Death, Society and Human Experience*, CV Mosby, St Louis

——1988, 'Safe death in the postmodern world', in *A Safer Death: Multidisciplinary Aspects of Terminal Care*, eds A Gilmore & S Gilmore, Plenum Press, New York

——1993a, 'Reconstructing death in postmodern society', *Omega*, vol. 27, no. 1, pp. 75–89

——1993b, 'Dame Cicely Saunders: an Omega interview', *Omega*, vol. 27, no. 4, pp. 263–9

Kastenbaum, R & Thuell, S 1995, 'Cookies baking, coffee brewing: toward a contextual theory of dying', *Omega*, vol. 31, no. 3, pp. 175–87

Katz, J & Sidell, M 1994, *Easeful Death: Caring for Dying and Bereaved People*, Hodder & Stoughton, London

Kearl, M 1995, 'Death and politics: a psychological perspective', in *Dying: Facing the Facts*, 3rd edn, eds H Wass & R Neimeyer, Taylor & Francis, Washington

——1996, 'Dying well: the unspoken dimension of aging well', *American Behavioural Scientist*, vol. 39, no. 3, pp. 336–60

Keizer, B 1996, *Dancing With Mister D: Notes on Life and Death*, Doubleday, London

Kellehear, A 1984, 'Are we a "death-denying" society? A sociological review', *Social Science and Medicine*, vol. 18, no. 9, pp. 713–23

——1990, *Dying of Cancer: The Final Year of Life*, Harwood, London

——1994, 'The social inequality of dying', in *Just Health: Inequality in Illness, Care and Prevention*, eds C Waddell & A Petersen, Churchill Livingstone, Melbourne

——1996, *Experiences Near Death: Beyond Medicine and Religion*, Oxford University Press, New York

——1999, *Health Promoting Palliative Care*, Oxford University Press, Oxford

Kelly, M & Field, D 1996, 'Medical sociology, chronic illness and the body', *Sociology of Health and Illness*, vol. 18, no. 2, pp. 241–57

Kelner, M & Bourgeault, I 1993, 'Patient control over dying: responses of health care professionals', *Social Science and Medicine*, vol. 36, no. 6, pp. 757–65

Kirmayer, L 1988, 'Mind and body as metaphors: hidden values in biomedicine', in *Biomedicine Examined*, eds M Lock & D Gordon, Kluwer Academic Publishers, Dordrecht

Kissane, DW, Street, A & Nitschke, P 1998, 'Seven deaths in Darwin: case studies under the *Rights of the Terminally Ill Act*, Northern Territory, Australia', *Lancet*, vol. 352, no. 9134, pp. 1097–102

Kitchener, BA 1998, 'Nurses' attitudes to active voluntary euthanasia: a survey in the ACT', *Australian and New Zealand Journal of Public Health*, vol. 22, no. 2, pp. 276–8

Kleinman, A 1980, *Patients and Healers in the Context of Culture: An Exploration of the Borderland Between Anthropology, Medicine and Psychiatry*, University of California Press, Berkeley

——1988, *The Illness Narratives: Suffering, Healing and the Human Condition*, Basic Books, New York

——1992, 'Local worlds of suffering: an interpersonal focus for ethnographies of illness experience', *Qualitative Health Research*, vol. 2, no. 2, pp. 127–34

——1995, *Writing at the Margin: Discourse Between Anthropology and Medicine*, University of California Press, Berkeley

Koenig, B 1988, 'The technological imperative in medical practice: the social creation of a "routine" treatment', in *Biomedicine Examined*, eds M Lock & D Gordon, Kluwer Academic, Dordrecht

Komesaroff, P, Norelle Lickiss, J, Parker, M & Ashby, M 1995, 'The euthanasia controversy: decision making in extreme cases', *The Medical Journal of Australia*, vol. 162, no. 11, pp. 594–7

Kubler-Ross, E 1969, *On Death and Dying*, Macmillan, New York

——1975, *Death the Final Stage of Growth*, Prentice Hall, New Jersey

Kuhse, H, Singer, P, Baume, P, Clark, M & Rickard M 1997, 'End-of-life decisions in Australian medical practice', *The Medical Journal of Australia*, vol. 166, no. 4 pp. 191–6

Kutner, JS, Steiner, JF, Corbett, KK, Jahnigen, DW & Barton, PL 1999, 'Information needs in terminal illness', *Social Science and Medicine*, vol. 48, no. 10, pp. 1341–52

Kuupelomaki, M & Lauri, S 1998, 'Cancer patients' reported experiences of suffering', *Cancer Nursing*, vol. 21, no. 5, pp. 364–9

Le Shan, L 1977, *You Can Fight For Your Life*, M Evans & Company, New York

Levi, F, Lucchinin, F, La Vecchia, C & Negri, E 1999, 'Trends in mortality from cancer in the European Union', *Lancet*, vol. 354, no. 9180, pp. 742–3

Levin, R 1999, 'Cancer and the self: how illness constellates meaning', in *Health Studies: A Critical and Cross-Cultural Reader*, ed. C Samson, Blackwell, Oxford

Little, M, Jordens, C & Paul, K 1998, 'Liminality: a major category of the experience of cancer illness', *Social Science and Illness*, vol. 47, no. 10, pp. 1485–94

Littlewood, J 1993, 'The denial of death', in *The Sociology of Death*, ed. D Clark, Blackwell, Oxford

Lock, M 1996, 'Death in technological time: locating the end of meaningful life', *Medical Anthropology Quarterly*, vol. 10, no. 4, pp. 575–600

Lofland, J 1996, *Social Movement Organisation: Guide to Research on Insurgent Realities*, Aldine de Gruyter, New York

Logue, B 1994, 'When hospice fails: the limits of palliative care', *Omega*, vol. 29, no. 4, pp. 291–301

Lowenthal, R 1989, 'Can cancer be cured by meditation and "natural therapy"? A critical review of the book *You Can Conquer Cancer* by Ian Gawler', *The Medical Journal of Australia*, vol. 151, no. 11–12, pp. 710–15

Lundin, S & Akesson, L eds 1996, *Bodytime: On the Interaction of Body, Identity and Society*, trans. A Crozier, Lund University Press, Stockholm

Lupton, D 1994, *Medicine as Culture: Illness, Disease and the Body in Western Societies*, Sage, London

——1995, *The Imperative of Health: Public Health and the Regulated Body*, Sage, London

Lynam, J M 1990, 'Examining support in context: a redefinition from the cancer patient's perspective', *Sociology of Health and Illness*, vol. 12, no. 2, pp. 169–94

MacDonald, N 1993, 'Priorities in education and research in palliative care', *Palliative Medicine*, vol. 7, suppl. 1, pp. 65–76

MacDonald, WL 1998, 'Situational factors and attitudes toward voluntary euthanasia', *Social Sciences and Medicine*, vol. 46, no. 1, pp. 73–81

Maddocks, I 1990, 'Changing concepts in palliative care', *The Medical Journal of Australia*, vol. 152, no. 10, pp. 535–45

——1994, 'A new society of palliative medicine', *The Medical Journal of Australia*, vol. 160, no. 11, p. 670

——1999, 'Medicine and palliative care: shifting the paradigm', *The Medical Journal of Australia*, vol. 171, no. 2, pp. 63–4

Maeve, MK 1998, 'Weaving a fabric of moral meaning: how nurses live with suffering and death', *Journal of Advanced Nursing*, vol. 27, no. 6, pp. 1136–42

Marcus, G & Fischer, M 1986, *Anthropology as Cultural Critique*, University of Chicago Press, Chicago

Mathieson, C & Stam, H 1995, 'Renegotiating identity: cancer narratives', *Sociology of Health and Illness*, vol. 17, no. 3, pp. 283–306

McInerney, F 2000, '"Requested death": a new social movement', *Social Science and Medicine*, vol. 50, pp. 137–54

McKeown, T 1979, *The Role of Medicine: Dream, Mirage or Nemesis?* Blackwell, Oxford

McNamara, B, Waddell, C & Colvin, M 1994, 'The insitutionalisation of the Good Death', *Social Science and Medicine*, vol. 39, no. 11, pp. 1501–8

——1995, 'Threats to the good death: the cultural context of stress and coping among hospice nurses', *Sociology of Health and Illness*, vol. 17, no. 2, pp. 222–44

——1997, 'Five challenges to the good death in hospice', in *Meeting the Health Challenges of the 21st Century: Partnerships in Social Science and Health Science*, ed. V Miralao, The University of Philippines Press, Quezon City

McNamara, B, Martin, K, Waddell, C & Yuen, K 1997, 'Palliative care in a multicultural society: perceptions of health care professionals', *Palliative Medicine*, vol. No. 11, pp. 359–67

——1998, 'Ethnic diversity in dying, death and bereavement and the delivery of culturally appropriate care', unpublished report

Medicus, 1999, 'Helping doctors to help the dying', vol. 39, no. 7, p. 18

Mellor, P 1993, 'Death in high modernity: the contemporary presence and absence of death', in *The Sociology of Death*, ed. D Clark, Blackwell, Oxford

Mellor, P & Schilling, C 1993, 'Modernity, self-identity and the sequestration of death', *Sociology*, vol. 27, no. 3, pp. 411–31

Melucci, A 1989, *Nomads of the Present: Social Movements and Individual Needs in Contemporary Society*, Temple University Press, Philadelphia

Mesler, M 1995, 'The philosophy and practice of patient control in hospice: the dynamics of autonomy versus paternalism', *Omega*, vol. 30, no. 3, pp. 173–89

Metcalf, P and Huntington, R 1991, *Celebrations of Death: The Anthropology of Mortuary Ritual*, Cambridge University Press, Cambridge

Mitchell, J 1998, 'Cross-cultural issues in the disclosure of cancer', *Cancer Practice*, vol. 6, no. 3, pp. 153–60

Mitchell, K, Kerridge, I & Lovat, T 1996, *Bioethics and Clinical Ethics for Health Professionals*, 2nd edn, Social Science Press, Wentworth Falls

Moller, D 1990, *On Death Without Dignity: The Human Impact of Technological Dying*, Baywood, New York

Molloy, W & Clarnette, R 1993, *Let Me Decide: The Health Care Directive That Speaks for You When You Can't*, Penguin, Ringwood

Molloy, W & Guyatt, G 1991, 'A comprehensive health care directive in a home for the aged', *Canadian Medical Association Journal*, vol. 145, no. 4, pp. 307–11

Mor, V, Greer, D & Kastenbaum, R 1989, *The Hospice Experiment*, John Hopkins University Press, Baltimore

Mulkay, M 1993, 'Social death in Britain', in *The Sociology of Death*, ed. D Clark, Blackwell, Oxford

Muller, J 1994, 'Anthropology, Bioethics, and Medicine: A Provocative Trilogy', *Medical Anthropology Quartlely*, vol. 8, no. 4, pp. 448–67

Muller, J & Koenig, B 1988, 'On the boundary of life and death: the definition of dying by medical residents', in *Biomedicine Examined*, eds M Lock & D Gordon, Kulwer Academic, Dordrecht

Murphy, R 1987, *The Body Silent*, Phoenix House, London

Muzzin, LJ, Anderson, NL & Figueredo, AT 1994, 'The experience of cancer', *Social Science and Medicine*, vol. 38, no. 9, pp. 1201–8

New South Wales Cancer Council 1996 *Cancer in New South Wales: Incidence and Mortality*, NSWCC, Sydney

Nimocks, M, Webb, L & Connell, J 1987, 'Communication and the terminally ill: a theoretical model', *Death Studies*, vol. 11, no. 5, pp. 323–44

Nuland, S 1993, *How We Die*, Chatto & Windus, London

Palgi, P & Abramovitch, H 1984, 'Death: a cross-cultural perspective', *Annual Review of Anthropology*, vol. 13, pp. 385–417

Pappas, D 1996, 'Euthanasia and assisted suicide: are doctors' duties when following patients' orders a bitter pill to swallow?' in *Contemporary Issues in the Sociology of Death, Dying and Disposal*, eds G Howarth & P Jupp, Macmillan, London

Parkes, CM 1978, 'Psychological aspects', in *The Management of Terminal Disease*, ed. C Saunders, Edward Arnold, London

Payne, S, Langley-Evans, A & Hillier, R 1996, 'Perceptions of a "good" death: a comparative study of the views of hospice staff and patients', *Palliative Medicine*, vol. 10, no. 4, pp. 307–12

Pearce, I & Findlay, R 1987, *The Holistic Approach to Cancer*, Boturich, Dunbartonshire

Pearlin, L 1989, 'The sociological study of stress', *Journal of Health and Social Behaviour*, vol. 30, pp. 241–56

Petersen, A 1994, *In A Critical Condition: Health and Power Relations in Australia*, Allen & Unwin, Sydney

Petersen, A & Lupton, D 1996, *The New Public Health: Health and Self in an Age of Risk*, Allen & Unwin, Sydney

Perakyla, A 1991, 'Hope work in the care of seriously ill patients', *Qualitative Health Research*, vol. 1, no. 4, pp. 407–33

Pinell, P 1987, 'How do cancer patients express their points of view?', *Sociology of Health and Illness*, vol. 9, no. 1, pp. 25–44

Pisani, P, Parkin, DM, Bray, F & Ferlay, J 1999, 'Estimates of the worldwide mortality from 25 cancers in 1990', *International Journal of Cancer*, vol. 83, no. 1, pp. 18–29

Plante, A & Bouchard, L 1996, 'Occupational stress, burnout, and professional support in nurses working with dying patients', *Omega*, vol. 32, no. 2, pp. 93–109

Pollock, K 1993, 'Attitude of mind as a means of resisting illness', in *Worlds of Illness: Biographical and Cultural Perspectives on Health and Disease*, ed. A Radley, Routledge, London

Porter, R & Porter, D 1988, *In Sickness and in Health: The British Experience 1650–1850*, Fourth Estate, London

Prior, L 1989, *The Sociological Organisation of Death*, Macmillan, Hampshire

Quint Benoliel, J & Degner, L 1995, 'Institutional dying: a convergence of cultural values, technology, and social organisation', in *Dying: Facing the Facts*, eds H Wass & R Neimeyer, Taylor & Francis, Washington

Quirk, P 1998, 'Euthanasia in the Commonwealth of Australia', *Issues in Law and Medicine*, vol. 13, no. 4, pp. 425–46

Ramsay, P 1975, 'The indignity of death with dignity', in *Death Inside Out: The Hastings Centre Report*, eds P Steinfels & R Veatch, Harper & Row, New York

Reeves, GK, Beral, V, Bull, D & Quinn, M 1999, 'Estimating relative survival among people registered with cancer in England and Wales', *British Journal of Cancer*, vol. 79, no. 1, pp. 11–22

Rinaldi, A & Kearl, M 1990, 'The hospice farewell: ideological perspectives of its professional practitioners', *Omega*, vol. 21, no. 4, pp. 283–300

Robbins, M 1997, 'Assessing needs and effectiveness: is palliative care a specialist case?', in *New Themes in Palliative Care*, eds D Clark, J Hockley & S Ahmedzai, Open University Press, Buckingham

Robinson, B 1998, 'Euthanasia and physician-assisted suicide: all sides', http://www.religioustolerance.org/euthanas.htm#poll

Rose, J 1997, 'Australia overturns a law permitting it', *Medical Economics*, vol. 74, no. 10, p. 41

Roy Morgan Research Centre 1996, *Australians continue to support euthanasia as MPs discuss conscience vote (Finding No. 2933)*, Roy Morgan Research Centre, Melbourne

Russell, P & Sander, R 1998, 'Palliative care: promoting the concept of healthy death', *British Journal of Nursing*, vol. 7, no. 5, pp. 256–61

Saclier, A 1976, 'Good death: responsible choice in a changing society', *Australian and New Zealand Journal of Psychiatry*, vol. 10, no. 3, pp. 3–6

Salisbury, C, Bosanquet, N, Wilkinson, E, Franks, P, Kite, S, Lorentzon, M & Naysmith, A 1999, 'The impact of different models of specialist palliative care on patients' quality of life: a systematic literature review', *Palliative Medicine*, vol. 13, no. 1, pp. 3–17

Saunders, C & Baines, M 1983, *Living With Dying: The Management of Terminal Disease*, Oxford University Press, Oxford

Samson, C 1999, 'Disease and the self', in *Health Studies: A Critical and Cross-Cultural Reader*, ed. C Samson, Blackwell, Oxford

Saunders, C 1993, 'Some challenges that face us', *Palliative Medicine*, vol. 7, suppl. 1, pp. 77–83

Schneidman, E 1984, *Death: Current Perspectives*, Mayfield Publishing, Palo Alto

Schratz, M & Walker, R 1995, *Research as Social Change: New Opportunities for Qualitative Research*, Routledge, London

Seale, C 1989, 'What happens in hospices: a review of research evidence', *Social Science and Medicine*, vol. 28, no. 6, pp. 551–9

——1991, 'Communication and awareness about death: a study of a random sample of dying people', *Social Science and Medicine*, vol. 32, no. 8, pp. 943–52

——1995, 'Heroic Death', *Sociology*, vol. 29, no. 4, pp. 597–613

——1998, *Constructing Death: The Sociology of Dying and Bereavement*, Cambridge University Press, Cambridge

Seale, C & Addington-Hall, J 1994, 'Euthanasia: why people want to die earlier', *Social Science and Medicine*, vol. 39, no. 5, pp. 647–54

——1995, 'Euthanasia: the role of good care', *Social Science and Medicine*, vol. 40, no. 5, pp. 581–7

Seale, C & Cartwright, A 1994, *The Year Before Death*, Averbury, Aldershot

Seale, C, Addington-Hall, J & McCarthy, M 1997, 'Awareness of Dying: prevalence, causes and consequences', *Social Science and Medicine*, vol. 45, no. 3, pp. 477–84

Selye, H 1986, 'Cancer, stress and the mind', *Cancer, Stress and Death*, Plenum Medical Books, New York

Seymour, W 1998, *Remaking the Body: Rehabilitation and Change*, Allen & Unwin, Sydney

Siebold, C 1992, *The Hospice Movement: Easing Death's Pains*, Twayne Publishers, New York

Singer, PA, Choudhry, S & Armstrong, J 1995, 'Public opinion regarding end-of-life decisions: influence of prognosis, practice and process', *Social Science and Medicine*, vol. 41, no. 11, pp. 1517–21

Slomka, J 1992, 'The negotiation of death: clinical decision making at the end of life', *Social Science and Medicine*, vol. 20, no. 3, pp. 251–9

Small, N 1997, 'The impact of thanatology on the emerging hospice movement', Conference paper presented at The Social Context of Death, Dying and Disposal 3rd International Conference, University of Wales, Cardiff

Smith nd, 'Casemix in palliative care' in *The Practice of Palliative Care: Highlights of a Palliative Care Roundtable*, Tape recording provided by *Pharmacia*

Sontag, S 1978, *Illness as a Metaphor*, Farrar, Strus & Giroux, New York

——1989, *AIDS and its Metaphors*, Allen Lane, London

Spradley, J 1980, *Participant Observation*, Harcourt Brace Jovanovich College Publishers, Fort Worth

Stacey, J 1997, *Teratologies: A Cultural Study of Cancer,* Routledge, London

Stedeford, A 1984, *Facing Death: Patients, Families and Professionals,* William Heinemann Medical Books, London

Steinberg, MA, Najman, JM, Cartwright, CM, MacDonald, SM & Williams, GM 1997, 'End-of-life decision-making: community and medical practitioners' perspectives', *Medical Journal of Australia,* vol. 166, no. 3, pp. 131–5

Stevens, C & Hassan, R 1994, 'Management of death, dying and euthanasia: attitudes and practices of medical practioners in South Australia', *Journal of Medical Ethics,* vol. 20, no. 1, pp. 41–6

Stoddard, S 1978, *The Hospice Movement: A Better Way of Caring for the Dying,* Stein & Day, New York

Sudnow, D 1967, *Passing On: The Social Organisation of Dying.* Prentice-Hall, Englewood Cliffs

Sweeting, H & Gilhooly, M 1997, 'Dementia and the phenomenon of social death', *Sociology of Health and Illness,* vol. 19, no. 1, pp. 93–117

Taylor, B 1993a, 'Hospice nurses tell their stories about a good death: the value of storytelling as a qualitative health research method', *Annual Review of Health Social Science,* vol. 3, pp. 97–108

——1993b, 'What does a good death of people in their care mean to hospice nurses?', Paper presented at the National Hospice and Palliative Care Conference, Melbourne

Teno, JM, Stevens, M, Spernak, S & Lynn, J 1998, 'Role of written advance directives in decision making: insights from qualitative and quantitative data', *Journal of General Internal Medicine,* vol. 13, no. 7, pp. 439–46

Thompson, N 1997, 'Masculinity and loss', in *Death, Gender and Ethnicity,* eds D Field, J Hockey & N Small, Routledge, London

Thomsen, O, Wulff, H, Martin, A & Singer, P 1993, 'What do gastroenterologists in Europe tell cancer patients?', *Lancet,* vol. 341, no. 8843, pp. 773–6

Tilden, V & Gaylen, R 1987, 'Cost and conflict: the darker side of social support', *Western Journal of Nursing Research,* vol. 9, no. 1, pp. 9–18

Timmermans, S 1994, 'Dying of awareness: the theory of awareness contexts revisited', *Sociology of Health and Illness,* vol. 16, no. 3, pp. 322–39

Tocqueville, Alexis de 1945, *Democracy in America,* vol. 2, Vintage, New York

Turner, B 1984, *The Body and Society: Explorations in Social Theory,* 2nd edn, Sage, London

——1992, *Regulating Bodies,* Routledge, London

Turner, L 1998, 'An anthropological exploration of contemporary bioethics: the varieties of common sense', *Journal of Medical Ethics,* vol. 24, no. 2, pp. 127–33

Twycross, R 1993, 'Research and palliative care: the pursuit of reliable knowledge (editorial)', *Palliative Medicine,* vol. 7, no. 3, pp. 175–7

United States Census Bureau 1997, 'Population Profile of the United States', http://www.census.gov/prod/3/98pubs/p23–194.pdf

Vachon, M 1987, *Occupational Stress in the Care of the Critically Ill, the Dying, and the Bereaved,* Hemisphere Publishing, Washington

——1995, 'Staff stress in hospice/palliative care: a review', *Palliative Medicine,* vol. 9, no. 2, pp. 91–122

Van Gennep, A 1960, *The Rites of Passage,* trans. M Vizedom & G Caffee, University of Chicago Press, Chicago

Veatch, R 1976, *Death, Dying and the Biological Revolution: Our Last Quest for Responsibility,* Yale University Press, New Haven

Vigano, A, Dorgan, M, Bruera, E & Suarez-Almazor, ME 1999, 'The relative accuracy of the clinical estimation of the duration of life for patients with end of life cancer', *Cancer*, vol. 86, no. 1, pp. 170–6

Waddell, C, Clarnette, R, Smith, M, Oldham, L & Kellehear, A 1996, 'Treatment decision-making at the end of life: a survey of Australian doctors' attitudes towards patients' wishes and euthanasia', *The Medical Journal of Australia*, vol. 165, no. 10, pp. 540–4

Waddell, C, Clarnette, RM, Smith, M & Oldham, L 1997, 'Advance directives affecting medical treatment choices', *Journal of Palliative Care*, vol. 12, no. 2, pp. 5–8

Waddell, C & McNamara, B 1997, 'The stereotypical fallacy: a comparison of Anglo and Chinese Australians' thoughts about facing death', *Mortality*, vol. 2, no. 2, pp. 149–61

WA Hospice Palliative Care Association in collaboration with the Health Department of WA 1995, 'Palliative care in Western Australia to the year 2001'

Walder, J 1994, *My Breast: One Woman's Cancer Story*, The Woman's Press, London

Walter, T 1991, 'Modern death—taboo or not taboo?', *Sociology*, vol. 25, no. 2, pp. 293–310

——1994, *The Revival of Death*, Routledge, London

——1995, 'Natural death and the noble savage', *Omega*, vol. 30, no. 4, pp. 237–48

Weber, D 1995, 'Deathcare: exploring the troubled frontier between medical technology and human mortality', *Healthcare Forum Journal*, March/April, pp. 14–25

Weeks, JC, Cook, EF, O'Day, SJ, Peterson, LM, Wenger, N, Reding, D, Harrell, FE, Kussin, P, Dawson, NV, Connors, AF Jr, Lynn, J & Phillips, RS 1998, 'Relationship between cancer patients' predictions of prognosis and their treatment preferences', *Journal of the American Medical Association*, vol. 279, no. 21, pp. 1709–14

Weisman, A 1978, 'An appropriate death', in *Death and Identity: Challenge and Change*, eds R Fulton, E Markusen, G Owen & J Scheiber, Addison-Wesley, Reading

Weissman, D, Block, S, Blank, L, Cain, J, Cassem, N, Danoff, D, Foley, K, Meier, D, Schyve, P, Theige, D & Weeler, H 1999, 'Recommendations for incorporating palliative care education into the acute care hospital setting', *Academic Medicine*, vol. 74, no. 8, pp. 871–7

Wicks, D 1995, 'Nurses and doctors discourses of healing', *The Australian and New Zealand Journal of Sociology*, vol. 31, no. 2, pp. 122–39

Wiffen, P 1998, 'Evidence-based care at the end of life', *Palliative Medicine*, vol. 12, no. 1, pp. 1–3

Wilkes, E 1986, 'Terminal care: how can we do better?', *Journal of the Royal College of Physicians of London*, vol. 20, no. 3, pp. 216–18

Wilkinson, E, Salisbury, C, Bosanquet, N, Franks, P, Kite, S, Lorentzon, M & Naysmith, A 1999, 'Patient and carer preference for, and satisfaction with, specialist models of palliative care: a systematic review', *Palliative Medicine*, vol. 13, no. 3, pp. 197–216

Williams, R 1989, 'Awareness and control of dying: some paradoxical trends in public opinion', *Sociology of Health and Illness*, vol. 11, no. 3, pp. 201–12

Williams, S & Calnan, M eds 1996, *Modern Medicine: Lay Perspectives and Experiences*, UCL Press, London

Williamson, P 1996, *'Let Me Die In My Country': Palliative Care Needs of Aboriginal People in the Kimberley and Pilbara Regions in Western Australia*, Health Department, Western Australia

Willis, E 1983, *Medical Dominance: The Division of Labour in Australian Health Care*, Allen & Unwin, Sydney

——1994, *Illness and Social Relations: Issues in the Sociology of Health Care,* Allen & Unwin, Sydney

Wingo, PA, Ries, LA, Rosenberg, HM, Miller, DS & Edwards, BK 1998, 'Cancer incidence and mortality, 1973–1995: a report card for the US', *Cancer,* vol. 82, no. 6, pp. 1197–207

Winland-Brown, JE 1998, 'Death, denial, and defeat: older patients and advance directives', *Advanced Practice Nursing Quarterly,* vol. 4, no. 2, pp. 36–40

Wolff, J 1989, *The Science of Cancerous Disease from Earliest Times to the Present,* Amerind, New Delhi

World Health Organisation 1996, *World Health Statistics Annual,* Geneva

Wright, M 1981, 'Coming to terms with death: patient care in a hospice for terminally ill', in *Medical Work: Realities and Routines,* eds P Atkinson & C Heath, Gower, London

Yates, P, Beadle, G, Claverino, A, Najman, J, Thomson, D, Williams, G, Kenny, L, Roberts, S, Mason, B & Schlect, D 1993, 'Patients with terminal care who use alternative therapies: their beliefs and practices', *Sociology of Health and Illness,* vol. 15, no. 2, pp. 199–216

Young, M & Cullen, L 1996, *A Good Death: Conversations with East Londoners,* Routledge, London

Zlatin, D 1995, 'Life themes: a method to understand terminal illness', *Omega,* vol. 21, no. 3, pp. 189–206

Zola, I 1972, 'Medicine as an institution of social control', *Sociological Review,* vol. 20, pp. 487–504

Index

uncertainties surrounding, 34–5, 37
universal measure of, 5
see also good death; management of death/dying
death as a social phenomenon, 5–6, 42
death as a 'taboo' topic, 81–2, 113
death awareness contexts, 25, 44
'death awareness' movement, 3, 82
death certificate, 8
death rituals, 68–9
decision-making
    cognitive impairment and, 58
    family, 65
    medical hierarchies and, 75–6, 104
    patient age and, 63
    shared, 45, 47
    socio-demographic variables affecting, 62
defining cause of death, 71–2
defining death, 72
defining good death, 46–8
degenerative disease, 71–2
    bodily deterioration and, 55–8
depression, 50
diagnosis, 80–1
    disclosing, 82–4, 87–8
    see also discussing death/dying
Diana, Princess, 6, 69
disclosure norms (palliative care), 88
discussing death/dying, 9, 14–16, 52, 80–1, 113, 125
    awareness contexts for, 25, 44
    health professionals', 90–1
    multicultural survey, 84–5
    survey, 82–4
disease, 3, 11, 42
    biomedical model of, 73
    classifying patients, 38, 57
    degenerative, 71–2
    determining euthanasia debate, 21
    perceptions of different, 29
    see also cancer
Doctor Death, 16
doctors, 78
    communicating bad news, 81, 87
    euthanasia stance, 17

god-like role of, 74
inadequacy of, 79
power play amongst, 75–6, 104
Dutch Criminal Code, 16
dying, 54, 72
    as a part of life, 4, 135
    as a social problem, 1–4
    'baby boomers' knowledge of, 3
    challenge of, 2
    privatisation of, 6–7
    process of, 35–7, 72, 84
    prolonged, 3, 7, 11, 52
    secrecy about, 12
    social process of, 5
    uncertainties surrounding, 34–5, 37
    see also terminally ill people

end-of-life matters, 15, 18
    advance directives, 18–20
    wills, 44
Enlightenment period, 68, 70
ethnography, 136, 141–2
    analysis, 140
    fieldwork, 137–40
    surveys, 143
euthanasia, 4, 8, 11, 21–3, 82, 143
    Alzheimer's disease debate, 20–1
    as a 'good death', 43
    Australian experiment, 16–17, 78
    Janet Mills, 23
    Netherlands and, 16
    patient interviews, 21–2
    public support for, 17
    requests, 98–9
    survey, 20
    terminal sedation and, 105–6
evangelicalism, 20
examples see cases/examples/interviews

failure of the body, 55–8
family
    care, 64–5, 100
    composition of, 81
    non-English speaking, 86
fatalism and cancer, 32–3
fatigue, 56